Conceptualizing Child–Adult Relations

Conceptualizing Child–Adult Relations focuses on how children conceptualize and experience child–adult relations. The authors explore the idea of generation as a key to understanding children's agency in intersection with social worlds, which are largely organized and ordered by adults. Within this broad theme, the authors explore two interconnected themes: how children define the division of labour between children and adults, and how far children regard themselves as constituting a separate social group.

Through study of how children understand their childhoods in generational contexts, this book uses information from children as a means to understand the social phenomenon of childhood. *Conceptualizing Child–Adult Relations* brings together researchers exploring these understandings in an unusually wide range of societies – the UK, Finland, Switzerland, Australia, Germany, Bolivia and Outer Mongolia. Their studies reveal the similarities and diversity of children's understanding of their social status and adult expectations of how they should live their lives. This allows for consideration of a range of childhoods and of how social factors shape, or intersect, with the character of these childhoods.

This book is ground-breaking in its focus on the variety and commonality in children's lives and views across a broad range of contexts. It provides innovative theoretical approaches to the growing study of childhood by homing in on intergenerational relations as a main concept, and draws attention to links across the main sites of children's lives such as the home, neighbourhood and school. Moreover, for policy-related issues, this book provides food for thought about the social conditions and status of childhood, and the factors structuring it.

Leena Alanen is a sociologist and Professor at the Department of Early Childhood Education, University of Jyväskylä. She is currently President of the Research Committee 53: Sociology of Childhood (International Sociological Association). **Berry Mayall** is Professor of Childhood Studies at the Social Science Research Unit, University of London's Institute of Education.

Future of Childhood Series
Series Editor: Alan Prout

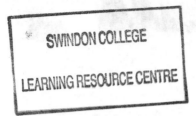

Conceptualizing Child–Adult Relations
Edited by Leena Alanen and Berry Mayall

Children, Technology and Culture: The Impacts of Technologies in Children's Everyday Lives
Edited by Ian Hutchby and Jo Moran-Ellis

Hidden Hands: International Perspectives on Children's Work and Labour
Edited by Chris Pole, Phillip Mizen and Angela Bolton

Conceptualizing Child–Adult Relations

Edited by Leena Alanen and
Berry Mayall

London and New York

First published 2001 by RoutledgeFalmer
2 Park Square, Milton Park, Abingdon, Oxon OX14 4RN

Simultaneously published in the USA and Canada
by RoutledgeFalmer
270 Madison Avenue, New York, NY 10016

RoutledgeFalmer is an imprint of the Taylor & Francis Group

© 2001 Leena Alanen and Berry Mayall for selection and editorial
matter; individual contributors their contribution

Typeset in Bembo by
J&L Composition Ltd, Filey, North Yorkshire

British Library Cataloguing in Publication Data
A catalogue record for this book is available
from the British Library

Library of Congress Cataloging in Publication Data
Conceptualizing child-adult relations/Leena Alanen and
Berry Mayall.
    p. cm.
    Includes bibliographical references and index.
    1. Children and adults.   2. Parent and child.
    I. Alanen, Leena.   II. Mayall, Berry.
BF723.P25 C65 2001
305.23–dc21   00-045953

ISBN 0-415-23159-0 (pbk)
       0-415-23158-2 (hbk)

Contents

List of illustrations

Figures

Tables

Notes on contributors

Leena Alanen works in the Department of Early Childhood Education, University of Jyväskylä. She was the Finnish representative on the international programme Childhood as a Social Phenomenon (1987–92) and is President of the Research Committee 53: Sociology of Childhood (International Sociological Association). She has published in the field of childhood research in Finnish, Swedish, German and English. Recent publications in English include: 'Rethinking childhood', *Acta Sociologica* 1988; 31: 53–67; 'Gender and generation: feminism and "the child question"', in J. Qvortrup *et al.* (eds) *Childhood Matters*, Aldershot: Avebury Press, 1994; and 'Children and the family order: constraints and competences', in I. Hutchby and J. Moran-Ellis (eds) *Children and Social Competence: Arenas of Action*, London: Falmer, 1998.

Pia Christensen works at the University of Hull and teaches in Childhood Studies at the South Jutland University Centre, Denmark. She has researched children as social actors in the context of Danish schools, with particular reference to children's care-giving activities. She worked with Allison James and Chris Jenks on 'Changing Times: Children's Understanding and Perception of the Social Organisation of Time' (one of twenty-two projects on the ESRC Children 5–16 Programme). Recent publications include: 'Difference and similarity: how children's competence is constituted in illness and its treatment', in I. Hutchby and J. Moran-Ellis (eds) *Children and Social Competence*, London: Falmer, 1998; 'Children and vulnerability', in A. Prout (ed.) *Children, Society and the Body*, London: Macmillan, 2000; and P. Christensen and A. James (eds) *Research with Children*, London: Falmer, 2000.

Jan Falloon is a teacher and manager in the Childhood and Youth Policy Research Unit, Faculty of Arts and Social Sciences, University of Western Sydney, Australia.

Allison James works at the School of Comparative and Applied Social Sciences at the University of Hull. Her work in collaboration with Alan Prout and Chris Jenks has been seminal in developing the sociology of childhood in the UK. Her most recent empirical study, with Pia Christensen and Chris Jenks, is into children's understanding and perception of the social organization of children's time (one of twenty-two projects on the ESRC Children 5–16 Programme). Recent publications include: A. James and A. Prout (eds) *Constructing and Reconstructing Childhood*, London: Falmer, 1990/97; *Childhood Identities: Self and Social Relationships in the Experience of the Child*, Edinburgh: Edinburgh University Press, 1993; and with C. Jenks and A. Prout, *Theorising Childhood*, Cambridge: Polity, 1998.

Jan Mason works at the Childhood and Youth Policy Research Unit, Faculty of Arts and Social Sciences, University of Western Sydney, Australia. Recent relevant publications include: (ed.) *Child Welfare Policy: Critical Australian Perspectives*, Sydney: Hale & Iremonger, 1993; 'Privatisation and substitute care: recent policy developments in New South Wales and their significance', *Children Australia* 1996; 21: 4–8; and with B. Steadman, 'The conceptualisation of childhood and its implications for child protection policy', *Family Matters* 1997; 46: 31–6.

Berry Mayall is Professor of Childhood Studies at the Social Science Research Unit, Institute of Education, University of London. From 1991 to 1993, she ran the first UK national seminar group on childhood studies. She has worked since 1990 on research projects with children. Her most recent empirical study is 'Negotiating Childhoods' (one of twenty-two projects on the ESRC Children 5–16 Programme), and she is currently writing a book on that and her earlier studies. Recent publications include: (ed.) *Children's Childhoods: Observed and Experienced*, London: Falmer, 1994; *Children, Health and the Social Order*, Milton Keynes: Open University Press, 1996; 'Towards a sociology of child health', *Sociology of Health and Illness* 1998; 20: 269–88.

Cléopâtre Montandon studied social anthropology at Columbia University, New York, and currently works at the Faculty of Psychology and the Social Sciences, University of Geneva. Her main research interests have been the study of socialization, deviance and the sociology of childhood. Recent publications include: with F. Osiek, *L'Éducation du point de vue des enfants*, Paris: L'Harmattan, 1997; 'Processus de socialisation et vécu émotionnel des enfants', *Revue Française de Sociologie* 1996; 37: 263–85; 'Children's perspectives on their education', *Childhood* 1998; 5: 247–63; and 'Le point de vue des enfants sur la construction des liens sociaux: l'exemple de la violence contre les élèves', *Revue Suisse de Sociologie* (forthcoming).

Helen Penn works on early childhood studies at the University of East London. She has experience as an administrator in local authority provision of early years services, and is much in demand worldwide as a consultant on the development of such services. Her current research work focusses on the ideologies, character and quality of early years services in a range of countries. Recent publications include: *Comparing Nurseries: The Experiences of Children and Staff in Day Nurseries in Spain, Italy and the UK*, London:

Paul Chapman, 1997; *Policy Review of Early Childhood Services in Developing and Transitional Countries,* London: Department for International Development, 1997; and (ed.) *Early Childhood Services: Theory, Policy and Practice,* Milton Keynes: Open University Press, 2000.

Alan Prout, Series Editor, is Professor of Sociology at Stirling University and Director of the Economic and Social Research Council's Children 5–16 Research Programme.

Samantha Punch has conducted ethnographic research on children's lives in rural Bolivia, and on young people's problems and coping strategies in Scotland ('Pathways to Welfare': one of twenty-two projects on the ESRC Children 5–16 Programme). She is currently carrying out research on children's experiences of sibling relationships and birth order in the UK at the Department of Applied Social Science, University of Stirling. Recent publications include: 'Children's strategies for creating playspaces: negotiating independence in rural Bolivia', in S. Holloway and G. Valentine (eds) *Children's Geographies: Living, Playing, Learning and Transforming Everyday Worlds,* London: Routledge, 2000; and 'Multiple methods and research relations with children in rural Bolivia', in M. Limb and C. Dwyer (eds) *Qualitative Methods for Geographers,* London: Arnold, forthcoming 2001.

Helga Zeiher is a research scientist at the Max Planck Institute for Human Development and Education, Berlin. Until 1999, she was Chair of the Sociology of Childhood section in the German Association of Sociology. Her main research interests have been the use of time and space in children's shaping of their daily life in family and peer relations. Recent publications include: H. J. Zeiher and H. Zeiher, *Orte und Zeiten der Kinder: Soziales Leben im Alltag von Grossstadtkindern* [Children's places and times: everyday social life of city children], Weinheim: Juventa, 1994; H. Zeiher, P. Buchner and J. Zinnecker (eds) *Kinder als Aussenseiter? Umbrüche in der gesellschaftlichen Wahrnehmung von Kindern und Kindheit* [Are children outside society?: changes in social perceptions of children and childhood], Weinheim: Juventa, 1996; 'Kinder und ihre Verwandten' [Children and their relatives], in M. Wagner and Y. Schutze (eds) *Verwandschaft,* Stuttgart: Enke, 1998; and H. Hengst and H. Zeiher (eds) *Die Arbeit der Kinder: Kindheitskonzept und Arbeitsteilung zwischen den Generationen* [Children's work: the concept of childhood and the intergenerational division of labour], Weinheim: Juventa, 2000.

Preface

Recent years have witnessed a significant and important growth in the 'new social study of childhood'. Although children were an object of scientific enquiry, and a target of governance, throughout the last century, discontent with prevailing frameworks of study came to the fore in its last decades. Though beyond the scope of this short Preface, the genesis of this movement is worthy of study itself. It would, for example, be interesting to consider the possibility that it was a response to changes in the way that childhood was actually being constructed in contemporary societies. Children are increasingly, though very unevenly, constituted as 'persons in their own right', *inter alia* through consumerism, demographic change and the dissemination of democratic norms. In these circumstances it becomes implausible to conceptualize them as passive products of socialization. At the same time, one's attention has been drawn, in part through the wide availability and accelerated circulation of images and information, to the diversity of the forms that childhood takes across time and place. In the face of this, it has become less possible to think of childhood as a unitary, universal and purely 'natural' entity.

'The new social studies' of childhood, with its emphasis on children as participants in, as well as outcomes of, social relations, is an international phenomenon. Though perhaps currently strongest in Europe, its practitioners are found throughout the industrialized and the developing countries. While most associated with sociology, it is multidisciplinary in range, with work taking place in psychology, anthropology, human geography and social history. It is also increasingly making links with policy and practice, finding much in common with, for example, the movement towards realizing children's participation rights or recognizing their importance in development programmes.

'The Future of Childhood' is a series, of which this is the first volume, that draws on and gives expression to this new international and multidisciplinary research on childhood. Further volumes will explore children's work, children and technology, children and family change, children and schooling, and children's voice in social policy. It is particularly fitting, however, that the first volume of the series should address the question of generational relations. It addresses a tension that has run through new approaches to childhood. In developing these it was important to establish the conceptual autonomy of childhood. While recognizing it as a phenomenon distributed across different contexts, it was crucial to establish childhood as possessing a specific problematic and to prise it out from the institutional contexts such as the family, schooling or welfare systems, within which it had been hidden. At the same time it was important to avoid constituting childhood as a narrow empirical field outside and adrift from general social theory and analysis. Treating childhood as a relational concept is crucial to working successfully within this tension. Understanding children from a generational perspective, which itself has several aspects, is an important contribution to this task. It can help to raise awareness of generation as a dimension of social organization, working alongside, in and between others such as class, gender and ethnicity. At the same time it can focus attention on the active process of (re)making generational relations across time and space. This volume takes an important step towards these tasks both by the acuteness of its theoretical discussion and by the richness of the empirical studies it makes available.

Alan Prout
Series Editor for The Future of Childhood

Acknowledgements

The Editors thank the contributors for their hard work. Special thanks to Liz Schmitz and to Susannah Downs for sterling work on putting the book together. The Editors are also grateful to Alan Prout for discussions on the introductory chapters and for the Preface.

1 Introduction

Berry Mayall

An edited collection . . .

A collaboration towards a book

This book has been some time in the making. Leena Alanen and Berry Mayall first began to plan it in early 1996 when they were both working at the Department of Child Studies, Linköping University in Sweden. Their discussions grew out of their previous work; Leena had taken part in the Nordic One Parent study, Berry in UK studies on children's lives at home and school. They shared an interest in the work of the Childhood as a Social Phenomenon project – Leena had worked on the Finnish report (Alanen and Bardy 1990). Out of these discussions came the idea for a book which drew on studies from a range of societies, both majority and minority, where a common thread was the collection of empirical data with children about their everyday lives. Such a collection of papers would be the basis for theoretical exploration of childhood.

As editors we wanted the book to develop through collaboration. This would allow us to provide a concerted effort towards conceptualising childhood as a relational concept; at more practical levels it could lead to some consistency across the chapters. We established an e-mail list of contributors to exchange information, and held meetings with individual contributors as convenient. We also held three group meetings: in Finland (summer 1998), in England (spring 1999), in Germany (autumn 1999). These contacts allowed us to understand each other's interest in the topic and to work towards some common ground. We were able to discuss draft chapters and to consider relationships between the chapters.

All the contributors are well established researchers, and all are interested in the 'new childhood studies'. They come from varying backgrounds as regards discipline or departmental siting, and their areas or fields of study vary. Between them they have allegiances or histories in anthropology, sociology, psychology, education studies and social policy work. But it is reasonable to say that the core discipline under-pinning this book is sociology.

Purposes of the book

In this book we aim to consider child–adult relations using data collected with children. In particular we aim to focus on generational issues in child–adult relations. In seeking to develop understandings of childhood as a relational concept, we may initially identify three interlinked components of the concept, which may help in the exploration of child–adult relations at local and larger-scale levels. In each component, notions of childhood are at issue, and within and across the three components, time past, present and future require to be taken into account.

Firstly, at local levels, individual children and adults must interrelate across age divisions, power inequalities and (in families) household norms and needs. On the latter, the interactions and negotiations may be understood within a framework of a common enterprise – the household and the well-being of household members. At school child–adult relationships in the present intersect with the formal purposes and informal customs of schools, established in the past and looking to the future. An issue that arises here is possible gaps or conflicts between young people's experience of their lives and the adult assignment of characteristics to them. Those called children may not – or not in all contexts – define themselves as children; and, as discussed in, for instance, Chapters 5 and 9, evidence of children's moral agency does not square with adult mistrust of children's moral competence. Children's notions of their own and family history, as well as children's present and future, are critical issues here.

Secondly, relationships are also constituted between social groups: the social group children and the social group adults interact across the generations. Here we may be centrally concerned with notions of 'childhood' and of 'adulthood'; how people understand these and the distinctions between them; how they construct, legislate for, or enact behaviour at group level between the two groups. These understandings have their roots in time past – which throw long shadows forward – and they are re-negotiated and transformed through interactions between the groups. For instance, in Chapter 7, Helen Penn gives a dramatic example of such transformations, using the case of Outer Mongolia. The interests of the social group children may differ from those of the social group adults; and the impacts of social policies and norms will vary as between those two broad groups. Social demands made of the social group children may focus on time future, as well as on time present (or on time present in relation to time future).

Thirdly, adults belong to a different generation from children. Adults, born at a point 20 to 40 years before their children, carry with them knowledge, assumptions and experience acquired during their trajectory through their lives, and influenced by social forces in operation during their life span to date. The impacts of time past are therefore an important focus of study here. Thus in Chapter 4, Helga Zeiher analyses the impacts of past understandings of motherhood (and of childhood) on children's childhoods in Berlin now. As a later generation, children have been subject to social forces belonging to a later historical period than the generation of their parents. One small example, from the UK, is the character of school experience, for social policies and practices on school-based education have changed dramatically since parents of school-age children went to school. Children seem more accepting of current education practices than their parents (Kelley, Mayall and Hood 1997). So, whilst interactions between adult social groups may also reflect differing histories, interactions and negotiations between children and adults may perhaps be regarded as characterised more profoundly by generational difference.

Developing theoretical ideas about such issues constitutes an important strand in childhood studies and we devote the next chapter to a theoretical analysis of key areas. In Chapter 2, Leena Alanen analyses the concept of generation and suggests generation as a system of relationships among social positions. Thus children and adults are the holders of specific social positions which are defined in relation to each other and are defined within specific social structures. For instance, the family generational structure is a nexus of connections between those assigned to 'child' and those assigned to 'parents'; and this nexus both affects the actions of the people holding these positions, and is affected by their actions. Within the structure of the school, similarly, the actions of 'children' or 'pupils' are affected by the complex of relations in force, as are the actions of 'teachers', and at the same time, that complex of relations is affected by the actions of the people acting within this generational structure.

These ideas about the significance of generation as a key concept for analysing childhood derive from the seminal work of Mannheim (1952 [1928]); for him a generation consists of people who are exposed (especially in youth – regarded as a formative period) to broadly the same set of historical, cultural and/or political events and movements. In some cases such a generation of people become what he terms a generational unit, where they not only share perspectives, but are aware that others share them, and then, in some cases work together (as for instance the French Impressionists). People refer to the 1968 generation as people (now moving towards old age) whose consciousness or identity was shaped at that time. In Britain, we may similarly think of 'Thatcher's children' (Pilcher and Wagg 1996) as a generation of people in Britain whose ideas and purposes were formed in relation to social movements in the 1980s.

In exploring the generational structures within which childhood (and adulthood) is continuously produced and lived, an essential component of one's understanding is that children are agents. That is, they are not merely 'actors' – people who do things, who enact, who have perspectives on their lives. They are also to be understood as agents whose powers, or lack of powers, to influence and organise events – to engage with the structures which shape their lives – are to be studied.

Like other books in this Falmer series on childhood, this one includes studies covering a range of societies. This range opens up possibilities for theoretical analysis across childhoods. As contributors it has required us to discuss both as individuals and in group meetings ways in which child-adult relations are understood and operationalised in varying social conditions. It allows us and our readers to re-assess our assumptions, by problematising the dominance of studies from 'western' societies. It also allows us to consider the appropriateness of any one conceptualisation of childhood (or generational relations) in each of the conditions studied.

The research studies

Chapters 3 to 10 each draw on an empirical study where data were collected with children. All the studies concern the daily lives of 'ordinary' children, and the chapters consider children's agency in intersection with the varying social contexts that shape the distribution of their time at home, out and about, and at school. The data are used to discuss generational relations – that is, we try to link up the empirical evidence of childhood's relations with adulthood, with the larger-scale social processes that may be thought to determine those relations.

Each chapter follows the same order. It starts with an introductory section outlining the social, historical, political processes which give rise to the researcher's interest in the topic. A discussion on theoretical issues follows. The empirical study and its methods are described. The chapter then presents study data and it ends with a discussion.

In Sam Punch's paper (Chapter 3), children's agency is seen through the ways they seek to control and organise their use of time and space, within the limitations of the specific social ordering of subsistence households in rural Bolivia. She describes parental expectations that children contribute to household economic and social welfare, in domestic work, animal-related work and agriculture. Parents assume that children have obligations and responsibilities. Children in turn understand their contributions as important and valuable. Thus child-adult relationships can be seen as reciprocal or inter-dependent. Sam's interest is also in what children make of these expectations; whether they, as studies in other societies argue, resist and negotiate. She shows that they do indeed have their own agendas and preferences for use of time and space; and that they employ strategies of various kinds in relation to the tasks they are asked to do: avoidance, coping, attempts at re-allocating the task.

Discussion of dependence, independence and interdependence in child-adult relationships is taken up by Helga Zeiher (Chapter 4). She describes intersections between changes in ideas about child-rearing and changes in the social situation of mothers in West Germany over the last third of the twentieth century. Alongside these developments, the mother as housewife has gradually lost its primary significance as women have entered paid (mainly part-time) employment. Taking up the intersections of these developments, Helga uses three case studies of families in West Berlin to analyse how children achieve their personal position in the inter-generational relationships of the household, by shaping their activities in the context of the demands, constraints and possibilities they face. Theoretically, the analysis centres on child-adult relationships understood within constellations of historical processes, that is, as cohort relationships.

Cléopatre Montandon (Chapter 5) takes a specific point in the history of child-adult relationships in her study of children's experience of parents as educators at a time when education law in the canton of Geneva expects public primary schools to complement 'family education' and parents to support the school's mission. Yet there is no consensus about the meaning of these terms. And whilst education reforms are based on 'child-centred' principles, children's lives are increasingly controlled and 'scholarised' out of school hours. Cléopatre reports here on children's thoughts, feelings and actions as regards the ways their parents educate them: their views on parental authority and control and the strategies they use to face parental demands; their responses to parental projects and plans for their futures; and their accounts of home-school relations. The chapter reveals complex intersections of past, present and future in children's lives; parental practices now derive from knowledge and experience as participants in earlier cohort learning; children's experiences now also intersect with their own and parents' expectations and wishes for their futures. Cléopatre notes too relationships between the diversity of children's home experience and the pluralism and rapid change of the wider society.

Developments in educational policy in England and Wales provide the social context for children's experiences of learning at school, discussed in Chapter 6 by Pia Christensen and Allison James. These developments, including a National Curriculum, regular testing and competition between schools for custom, have meant that time has become an increasingly scarce resource at school. Pia and Allison explore the critical importance for children and teachers of control over time-use in relation to the social organisation and experience of schooling. Drawing on structuration theory, they show how the 'school' can be understood as an institution in process rather than as a fixed site of constraint; and how the 'school' is contingent on the everyday decisions and actions of both adults and children. Whilst adults at school have more control over time-use and space-use than children do, yet children act as agents in influencing their own experience. The chapter shows how they employed 'time-shifting' strategies, whereby, through modifying their attitudes to the work, they could alter the tempo of the day.

The changing culture of education in the UK – a wealthy minority society – is taking place in the context of global competitiveness. Mongolia – a poor majority world country – provides another example showing how such large-scale forces impact on children's daily lives. Helen Penn (Chapter 7) describes how this traditionally nomadic and pastoralist society, a client-state of the Soviet Union from 1921 to 1990, is now coping with the collapse of a system where basic universalist health and veterinary services and education services were provided. Nowadays, the herders must pay for such services and they do so through building up their herds; the only resource for the increased level of animal-care is children. As Helen describes, decreasing proportions of children now go to school, and many for only short periods. But at school, they are beginning to be exposed to the competitive, individualistic assumptions of the minority world. Thus children are not only learning a pastoralist life in a subsistence economy, but negotiating ideological change, from communism to market rhetoric. Whilst children have traditionally been taught to be respectful and obedient to adults, they are now faced with powerful minority world images of freedom and choices dependent on material goods, which they do not have.

Children living in a subsistence economy may be unused to being asked their opinion; children in schools in many societies may be used to learning what they are told rather than participating in the construction of knowledge. Chapter 8 provides us with a dramatic case where children are commonly silent. In the minority world, discourses on child abuse, as Jan Mason and Jan Falloon explore, tend to be adult-centred; they are constructed without children's contributions. By pathologising 'abusers' in contrast to 'normal' adults and families, and by defining children as victims, these discourses effectively emphasise child protection policy as the control of deviancy. In this chapter, unusually, we hear the views of young people living in 'normal' families (in Sydney). In their view, child abuse is the use of adult power to control children; it is a component of 'normal' adult behaviour to children; and it is institutionalised through the legitimation of unequal power relations between adults and children. The focus of the group discussions on the specific topic, child abuse, provided the young people with the opportunity to expand their arguments on a critical issue for them: adults' unjust behaviour and children's complementary understanding that adults regard them as not yet fully human.

Inter-generational relations are the focus of Berry Mayall's study (Chapter 9), and, like the Sydney young people, her London sample stressed adult power and authority as essential components of these relations. She discussed with children how they understand the social status of childhood, parenthood and adulthood; and by asking them next to describe and discuss their daily lives, she sought to consider how well their (to some extent normative) accounts of childhood squared with their experiences. In particular, she found that children's experience of their moral status was highly ambivalent; they were routinely suspected and disbelieved, yet also expected to be responsible agents; and they displayed in their accounts their competence in the construction and maintenance of relationships, in managing school work and in carrying out household jobs and childcare work. A striking feature of London children's lives is the heavy restrictions placed by parents on their access to space outside the home and school. 'Traffic danger' and 'stranger danger' have become powerful factors here; the protection and exclusion of children and of childhood is taken to extremes, by comparison with many societies. This is the social context for the emphasis children put on their family as their principal source of comfort and happiness; and whilst to British ears that may seem obvious, a commentary on it is provided by Leena Alanen's discussion.

In Chapter 10, Leena discusses her study of children living in a suburb of a central Finnish town. Social policies here have ensured that almost all parents work full-time, that housing is clean, safe and easily managed, that a substantial free meal is provided at school, that safe routes are provided from home to school and around the neighbourhood. Unlike London children, these go to school unaccompanied by adults, and organise their own time after school – at home, in the neighbourhood, and in various activities. These are the contexts for Leena's analysis which shows that whilst all the children speak easily and warmly about family, friends, school and special interests, they divide up as to which of these domains is the main site of their activity and interest. Thus 'being a child' clearly means different things for children strong in each of the four domains; only the family children clearly identified themselves mainly as a child. Children whose allegiance was in the other domains had less to say about inter-generational issues. However, by dint of the material basis for their lives as dependents in adult-led households, all the children also occupied a distinct 'child' position.

Researching with children

Collecting data with children

This book provides instances of a wide range of methods of data collection. In each case, as they describe, the researcher/s worked towards methods and 'tools' as appropriate for the study aims, the topics under consideration and the social context within which data could or should be collected. For instance, Jan Mason and Jan Falloon aimed to tap into young people's knowledge and understanding of child abuse. This is a sensitive topic and it was particularly important to ask the young people to participate fully in considering methods and siting of data collection. They themselves chose the format of group discussions, the composition of the group and the familiar site of the home. By contrast, Helen Penn aimed to consider childhood in the social context of life in the Mongolian steppes; and given time-limits, language barriers, and the complexity of the topic, she collected data through a range of methods: observation, a commissioned autobiography, discussions with adults, and with children via an interpreter, through study of official documents and of the historical context. In the Genevan context, it was possible and appropriate to interview children at home, and then with renewed permission at school. Leena, but not Berry, could accompany children on walks around the neighbourhood, since strangers are differently understood in Finland as compared to England.

In all, the chapters add to the growing literature on methods of research with children (for instance, Hutchby and Moran-Ellis 1998b; Sinclair 1996; Christensen and James 2000). Between them they use the following: ethnographic methods – observation, participant and non-participant, informal discussions; collection of background data on historical and social context; autobiography; instruments or tools – such as time-use charts, photos, drawings, diaries, worksheets; group discussion; successive individual interviews; discussions in pairs; questionnaires.

The researched and the researcher

Researchers working within the new childhood studies paradigms try to maintain throughout the work the idea of the child as subject. The researcher can put to the children in all honesty the proposition that they are uniquely positioned to give evidence on their own lives – the character and quality of childhood, seen in relation to adulthood. Thus the researcher has some concerns in common with children; the research is a joint enterprise to explore such issues.

But the adult researcher has also some differing concerns compared to children. These occur at all stages of the research. The aim of advancing theory on how childhood may be understood as a permanent social feature of societies requires some careful preparatory ivory tower consideration of just how to go about the research study and how to collect data with children. The laudable aim of consulting children about methods may reduce the chances of getting funding (funders commonly like methods to be specified and costed). The good practice of checking back findings with children sometimes runs into timing problems, since children may be much older, and acquiring new statuses (for instance as teenagers) by the time the research findings are fit to report back; a researcher who showed videos of themselves to children one year later found that they resisted attempts to get them to comment on the activities of their younger selves (personal communication). The social context of discussions between academics is useful as a means of advancing theory, but is not conducive to the involvement of children.

These issues are particularly salient where the central aims of the research are at a remove from directly policy-related issues. This is not to say that such research has nothing to say to children, but it may be that in some cases the researcher's responsibility is to give recognition to the social condition of childhood and to the agency of children through making research results available to policy-makers and practitioners who work with children. The studies in this book are all concerned with the way large-scale policies and social movements shape childhoods, and with what children make of these childhoods. The studies explore and throw light on children's agency in constructing their lives, in acceptance, negotiation and resistance; in so doing these studies add to the developing adult understanding that children and childhood should be taken seriously as constituents of the social order.

Conclusions

Putting together research from different social contexts is useful for re-considering theory. At theoretical levels, what we are doing here is comparative research. Studying collaboratively the studies from a range of societies has allowed us to consider common ground in child-adult relations, and how these may best be theorised. It also acts as a corrective to easy assumptions based on 'western' societies only. So the inclusion of some more collectivist societies (as in Chapters 3, 7 and 10) alongside the more individualistic ones points both to commonality in child-adult relations (such as childhood's social, economic and political dependency on adulthood) but also to differences in how certain issues, for instance inter-dependency, are played out in the processes of the construction of childhoods. Theoretical, conceptual issues such as these need to be worked on to make ground for comparative childhood research on the empirical level.

The chapters all draw on fairly small-scale data-sets – a sample of children from a larger society. This is in contrast to studies which consider broad sweeping changes in the conditions of childhood (such as industrialisation, urbanisation, scholarisation). The use of such small-scale data-sets allows for the deconstruction of the broader issues; we can consider the character and weight of children's agency in dealing with these. For instance, we can consider what children make of being required to spend portions of the day in institutions called schools (for instance see in Chapter 6); how they manage daily life and and make the best of it in the context of parents' daily participation, out of the home, in work. We can also see how broad social movements work out in varying societies – thus on the scholarisation of childhoods, we see that Bolivian children's days are divided between school and household duties (Chapter 3); but Berlin children have few duties apart from those relating to school (Chapter 4); the divisions of labour in the two societies put differing emphases on child and adult domestic work.

As noted above, the work presented here can be seen as having a political dimension. The general points that emerge from studying children in action in a range of settings are not only their acceptance of their social positioning and their enjoyment of it, but also their sense of being subordinate, of adult oppression and their resistances to it (see, for instance, Chapters 5, 8 and 9). These manifest themselves in their critiques of child–adult relations, their identification of contradictions within their status, their accounts of negotiations, tactics and strategies. Much of this centres on their rights as people, especially to participation in decision-making, to leisure time, to adequate resources for an acceptable standard of living. This is where the enterprise of studying children as subjects of the research and as agents in the construction of their own lives feeds into political processes. Some of the work of including children and childhood within political debate can be done by adults on their behalf, as suggested in the discussion on methods above. There are many instances now of collaborative work between adults and children to advance their rights (e.g. Hart 1997; Boyden 1997: 223). As the broad parameters of social theory on childhood become clearer, these may be of use to children as researchers and campaigners; already the UN Convention on the Rights of the Child is proving useful as a basis for children's actions to secure their rights.

The privilege we have had of spending our time researching childhood carries with it a collective responsibility for indicating to our readers where we think the growth points in the sociology of childhood lie. These are offered in this book for others to take up and develop as they see fit. Such messages lie in suggestions made in the individual chapters, but perhaps more importantly in what comes through from consideration of all of them together. We the authors have tried to move debates on as regards child–adult relations, and more, later studies will add to knowledge. This book hopes to provide insights for advancing comparative research on childhoods in varying national, cultural and ethnic contexts. Theoretically we have tried to address what we have increasingly come to see as a key concept in childhood studies: generation. We hope others will take it up and extend it further, both within childhood studies, by extending the empirical focus to other areas and arenas of children's action than those studied in this book; and also in juxtaposition with generational studies in research, for instance, on youth or adulthood.

2 Explorations in generational analysis

Leena Alanen

Introduction

Sociologists in the field of childhood studies have recognized childhood as a thoroughly social phenomenon and have worked this notion into a number of different approaches in studying childhood. This chapter argues that what has not yet been recognized clearly enough is that childhood is an essentially *generational* phenomenon. In the main chapters of this book, child–adult relations are the central topic, therefore this is a most appropriate place also to raise the question of the many ways in which the notion of generation can be used – and across the chapters are in fact used – in the study of children's lives, and even in what ways the study of childhood is always embedded in one or another form of generational frame. This introductory chapter aims to explore such issues, in the hope of clearing some of the conceptual ground surrounding the sociological study of childhood.

'Generation' – the concept – and generational studies already exist in social analysis: they have a history of their own, and an identifiable place within the field. But this history lies at some distance from the developments of the new sociology of childhood, and the relationship between childhood studies and generational studies has remained vague, despite the many reminders made in recent years to sociologists of childhood – most recently, by Qvortrup (2000: 88) – of the fundamental importance of the concept of generation for the study of childhood.

The chapter starts by reviewing three different strands of working sociologically on childhood and the place that the notion of 'generation' takes within each of them. Next, the chapter takes up notions of generation as they have been used both in everyday life and in social science. Karl Mannheim's theory of generations is paramount here, and the work of many others following his line of thinking has led to the emergence of the new study field of 'generations and cohorts research'. However, Mannheim's 'legacy' (Pilcher 1994) is not exhausted by this strand of research, for the link from Mannheim's generations to class analysis offers another route to generational analysis. Particular forms of class (and gender) analysis within sociology are therefore examined more closely, as possible models for thinking also of childhood. This step finally leads to a proposal for a specifically *generational analysis* of childhood. The chapter ends by confirming that the present stage in the sociological study of childhood, and particularly the stage of its theorization, will benefit from considering generation as a socially constructed system of relationships among social positions in which children and adults are the holders of specific social positions defined in relation to each other and constituting, in turn, specific social (and in this case generational) structures.

'Generation' in the sociologies of childhood

Sociologies of children

During the last 10–15 years, sociologists of childhood have strongly argued for the value (for sociology) of studying children in their own right and from their own perspectives, and for implementing this value in sociological work by taking children as the units of research and focusing the study directly on children and their life conditions, activities, relationships, knowledges and experiences. In this research children are approached as social actors and participants in the social world, and also as participants in the formation of their own childhoods.

This sociology of children is an important sub-field in the new sociological work on childhood; at present it dominates the field quantitatively. Its specific approach to childhood is to start from concrete, living children as they are found acting and participating in their own particular social worlds. The notion of generation, it seems, has no vital part to play in organizing this approach: although for the purpose of the study children may well be identified as a generational grouping in distinction to other groupings (babies, young people, adults, the elderly), that identification does not add anything to the analytics of the approach. Also, studying children's relationships with and their experiences or views of other generational groupings fits well into the basic paradigm of the sociology of children. Such issues, however, are in principle no more and no less topical and interesting to study than are, for instance, children's relationships with or experiences and views of disabled people, people belonging to various ethnic groups, or any other issue of social difference, or in fact any social issue.

In the sociology of children, then, 'generation' and 'generational' remain descriptive notions which may be used but which have limited import to the main goal of understanding children's lives.

Deconstructive sociology of childhood

Discussions in social sciences around post-positivist methodologies and their (constructionist) implications for social research provide the ground for the second, deconstructive strand among present-day sociologies of childhood. Here the notions of the child, children and childhood are all viewed as discursive formations through which ideas, images and 'knowledges' of children and childhood are conveyed in society. Often incorporated in broader social models of action and cultural practices, they also provide cultural scripts and rationales for people (including children themselves) to act on and as children. The task of the sociologist is then to 'deconstruct' such formations – cultural ideas, images, models and practices of children and childhood.

In this deconstructive sociology of childhood, too, 'generation' and 'generational' serve merely as descriptive notions; within it, as in the sociology of children approach, generational notions have no particular analytical role to play. If they come into use at all, the way they are used and their inherent meanings need not differ in any way from the everyday senses of the terms.

Structural sociology of childhood

In contrast to these two sociologies, 'generation' becomes an analytical issue and a problem to work on when the childhood phenomenon is seen in a structural context. This is the intended focus in a structural sociology of childhood: now childhood is fixed as a (relatively) permanent element in modern social life, although for individual children childhood is a transient period of life. In this approach 'childhood' itself is a structural phenomenon – that is, both structured and structuring (e.g. Qvortrup 1994), comparable and analogous to the proto-sociological 'class' and the notion of 'gender' in the social sciences. Therefore also, a structural approach presents childhood as being in continuous interplay with class and gender (and other social structures), and as being constructed and reconstructed within their interplay. In a structural view, actual living children, each living through their own uniquely constructed childhoods, are not the immediate focus. They are of course there, but this time assembled under the socially formed category of childhood, and the task of the sociologist is now to link the empirical manifestations of childhood at the level of children's lives with their macro-level contexts, and to focus on the social structures and mechanisms as they may be found to 'determine' these manifestations and in this sense help to explain them.

'Generation', in this third approach to childhood, is the term that names the social (or macro-) structure that is seen to distinguish and separate children from other social groups, and to constitute them as a social category through the work of particular relations of division, difference and inequality between categories. Even today, however, the structural notion of generation is not widely used in studying childhoods. When it is, it is often used to promote the comparative study of childhood: to compare the social conditions and circumstances in which the members of the social category of children live to those of adults (or some other generational category), and thereby to generate (politically) significant insights into distributive justice and the actual quality of children's everyday lives (see for example Qvortrup 1994 and 2000; Saporiti 1994; Sgritta 1994).

The conclusion from this short and limited review of the three sociologies of children and childhood and the place that generation and/or the generational is given in each of them, is that not much place has yet been given. Yet the social worlds in which children live and act are, in the end, generationally structured, in that there exists in our kind of societies the practically effective (and in this sense real) category of 'children'. There is hard empirical evidence, both from everyday experiences and social research, to show that membership in this category – as well as in its counter-category of adults – does make huge differences to them in terms of activities, opportunities, experiences and identities, as well as the relationships between the generational categories. In this sense it can be said that the structural as well as relational complex of generation constitutes the social phenomenon of childhood, and therefore, investigations are needed into the specific generational structures that in the end provide the focus of our research: children and childhood.

Meanings of 'generation'

'Generation' in common parlance

As a term, generation is common currency in everyday speech, used in many senses and for a variety of purposes, as evidenced by references to children as the 'next generation' (of adults) or to 'this generation of children'. We identify ourselves and other people as members of different generations ('the '68 generation', 'my grandparents' generation') and thereby point to and make sense of both the differences that we observe between people of different age, and their interrelationships, in terms of exchange, solidarity, conflict or 'gaps' in mutual understanding. Also, by identifying people as members of particular generations we locate them in historical time, as when speaking of the 'War generation' – those who lived through the war years – or the 'War Children', meaning (in Finland) those children who during the war years were sent away from their homes and families to neighbouring countries to live, some of them never returning home.

'Generation': lineal descent

The Greek and Latin etymologies of the word imply genealogies and succession, and generations are frequently defined according to relational lines of descent (Jaeger 1977: 430; Corsten 1999: 250). The original meaning is linked to kinship: descent along family lineage[1] but the sense has been generalized to cover also 'social' descent so that people speak of, for instance, 'second generation sociologists' (Corsten 1999: 251). This is also the sense in which generation is used in historical research: to describe succession in 'collective history' (Jaeger 1977).

Mannheim's 'generation'

Such usages of 'generation' also circulate in sociological texts. But in scientific reviews on the field, Karl Mannheim is unanimously credited as the scholar who brought 'generation' into sociology, in his paper on the 'problem of generations' (Mannheim 1952 [1928]).[2] He worked out his notion of generations within a sociology of culture frame (Matthes 1985; Corsten 1999: 53). In this view, generations needed to be understood and investigated as cultural phenomena: in their formation in specific social and historical contexts. More specifically, Mannheim argued that generations are formed when members of a particular age-group (or cohort), during their youthful years, live through the same historical and social events and experience them as significant to themselves. Through this shared experience they come to develop a common consciousness, or identity, which can be observed particularly in the world view and the social and political attitudes of the age-group in question. World views and attitudes moreover tend to persist over the life-course of cohort members, making membership in the same generation easily identifiable to members themselves and to others later on.

In Mannheim's cultural sociology, generations grow out of age-groups (cohorts), but only under specific circumstances. His conceptualization of the formation of generations proceeds in three stages. Firstly, people born (or 'located') in the same period of social and historical time within a society are exposed to a specific range of social events and ideas. At this stage they can be identified as sharing a 'generational location'; here they are only a 'potential generation', which exists merely in the mind of the researcher, not for the group members, who are not linked through actual relationships.

Here Mannheim reflects on the analogy between class and generation, noting that the class position of an individual is a 'different sort of social category, materially quite unlike the generation but bearing a certain structural resemblance to it'.[3] He then extends the analogy to class and generational positions and sees both as 'an objective fact, whether the individual in question knows his class [generational] position or not, and whether he acknowledges it or not' (Mannheim 1952 [1928]: 289).

The second stage in the formation of generations involves the development of a shared interpretation of experiences and definition of situations among those who share a generational location: when this takes place, the 'potential generation' becomes an 'actual generation' – analogously, we can see, to the development of a class 'in itself' to a class 'for itself'. Thirdly, in some cases, the differentiation within 'actual generations' may lead to the formation of 'generational units', characterized by face-to-face interaction among its members and similar ways of reacting to the issues they meet as a generation (Mannheim 1952 [1928]: 290, 302–12; Corsten 1999: 253–5).

In summary, Mannheim conceptualizes generations as first socially and historically formed and then, once formed, as possibly exerting an influence in the course of events. Thus his aim was to propose his theory of generations as a theory of social change, or of 'intellectual evolution' (Mannheim 1952 [1928]: 281), in which particular culturally formed groups act as collective agents and (cultural) bearers of social transformation, based on the socialization of cohort members during their formative years of youth (Becker 1997: 9–10; cf. Mannheim 1952 [1928]: 292–308).[4]

Mannheim's legacy

For decades after the publication of his seminal essay (in 1928) there was not much treatment of the subject in sociology. Later, Mannheim's thinking did find some response but mainly in a few small sub-disciplines, such as the study of youth groups and youth cultures. Since the 1960s developments in a few specific areas of social research, such as social demography, life course analysis and gerontology, have taken a closer look at Mannheim's theory of generations and made use of it in their research. In this activity scholars sorted out some of the confusions found in earlier usages (including Mannheim's) of 'generation' and developed precise distinctions and conceptualizations useful for the empirical aims of research.[5] Specific new research programmes have evolved out of this activity and space has been made for the field of 'generations research' or, more accurately, 'cohorts and generations research' to emerge (Becker 1997).[6]

By now research on generations in the Mannheimian tradition has forged for itself a secure place within (empirical) social research. In this research, Mannheim's original emphasis on youth as the key period for making fresh contact with social life and forming generational experiences has remained strong. Sociologists of childhood may, for good reasons, question this continued stress on youth by asking: why is youth seen as the first age of interest here? Are not *children* the obvious fresh cohort entering social life and therefore capable of sharing experiences in historical time and place; that is, of becoming a generation in a true Mannheimiam sense? While there has been some criticism directed at generations research for its tendency to overlook cohorts who are living through their later years and their potential for generating specific generational experiences (Pilcher 1995: 24), similar criticism has not been made as to children. One plausible explanation for this curious omission lurks in Ryder's paper (1965: 851–2), where he writes about the model of socialization and development which dominated the literature on childhood of his time. He argues that as long as life is conventionally seen as 'a movement from amorphous plasticity through mature competence towards terminal rigidity', young children will be seen as being merely in a preparatory phase, whereas youth (and adults) will be considered to be participants in social life. The more recent sociological work on childhood would object to this view and bring forward evidence to the effect that children too are participants in social life and, therefore, the Mannheimiam frame is fully applicable in childhood research too.[7] When this is accepted, then the further Mannheimian question: 'Do children also form actual generational groups or units?' can be opened for investigation.

In summary, outside this generations and cohorts niche within the social science field very little attention has been given to generational issues. Nor have issues of 'age' been attended to, until recently and in a few cases. In the British context, Janet Finch (1986: 12) describes the use of age in ways that are theoretically informed and empirically rigorous as 'relatively uncharted territory'; and Jane Pilcher (1994: 482), notes that 'the neglect of the sociology of generations parallels the lack of attention paid to the social significance of age'. In the 1990s there has been a burgeoning of theorizing and research on age, Pilcher writes, lamenting that in this new activity there still is a lack of theorizing and research in terms of generations (1994: 482) – and she means theorizing and research in the Mannheimian tradition.[8]

Beyond Mannheim

There is however more to discover – or in fact rediscover – in 'generation', by going beyond the line of analysis that has followed from Mannheim's important work. In recent decades many social conditions to which also childhood has been compared – gender, class, 'race' or ethnicity, disability – have been submitted to a critical, deconstructive gaze, by first interpreting them as social constructions and then reconceptualizing and researching them from a number of theoretical (post-positivist) perspectives. In feminist/gender studies gender continues to be discussed and analyzed, and it is variously theorized as a material, social and/or discursive structure while (social) class, of course, through the history of sociology as a scientific discipline, provides a central concept for analyzing and explaining social divisions and structural inequalities. Both ethnic studies and disability studies are more recent fields of research; they bring into focus and redefine both 'race'/ethnicity and disability as socially constructed phenomena, and seek to generate theoretical perspectives for research on these particular social constructions of inequality and exclusion.[9]

There are good reasons to believe that similarly sociologists will learn more about childhood as a social and specifically *generational* (structural) condition by working on the notion as an analogue to class, gender, ethnicity or disability. The suggestion is that 'generation' needs to be brought into childhood studies and childhood needs to be brought into generational studies. Such an approach, moreover, needs to be one that also holds to the basic premiss of the new childhood studies: children's agency. The rest of this chapter aims to develop such a perspective.

From class and gender to generation

One useful bridge leading from Mannheim's notion of generation towards a more structural notion is found in his own mode of reasoning, for he uses class as an analogue to generation: his argument is grounded on the idea of a 'generational location' as the structural – and not merely metaphorical – equivalent of 'class location'. But it needs to be noticed that the meaning of class he refers to is of the Weberian kind, for he emphasizes the common location in the social and historical process, in defining membership of class and, analogously, of age–group, or in his terms, 'generation' (Mannheim 1952 [1928]: 291; cf. Corsten 1999: 253).

The Weberian sense of class is essentially defined by the class situation ('the probability of enjoying the benefits of material goods, gaining a position in life and inner satisfactions 'as a result of a relative control over goods and skills' (Weber 1968 [1922]: 302). A class merely means all those people who share a same class situation and, therefore, the same set of life-chances and of opportunities in property and employment markets (Turner 1999: 225; Crompton 1998: 57). An alternative definition of class (used in Marxist class analysis) exists to this 'market-based' definition: now classes are defined by the economic relations of production in which they stand towards each other. Both of these senses of class are relational, but later in this chapter it will be shown that generational analysis will benefit from paying attention to the difference between two kinds of relations that may exist between individuals and categories of individuals: *external* relations (existing, for instance, between Weberian classes) and *internal* relations (existing, for instance, between Marxist-defined classes). But there are even more insights to be gained for developing generational analysis by exploring forms of class analysis.

In explicating two differing models of explanatory analysis, the (Marxist) class analyst Wright (1996: 123–5; 1997: 1–2), distinguishes between 'independent variable' and 'dependent variable' disciplines. Class or gender analysis can be done in the first, 'independent variable' analysis mode: the idea then is to explore the relationships between class or gender – this is the 'independent variable' – and all sorts of other phenomena. In contrast, when class or gender phenomena are investigated as 'dependent variables', the idea is to look for any social, biological, psychological or cultural factors that can be understood to generate the gender or class phenomena in question. The former, independent variable case does not mean that all phenomena can be explained primarily in terms of class or gender; in many cases it will prove that it is not an important determinant at all. However, the analysis is based on the conviction that class/gender is in many cases a pervasive social cause and therefore worth exploring in its ramifications for a variety of local phenomena.

It seems clear to me that Mannheim did not develop his form of generational analysis to fit into the former, 'independent variable' discipline. He did not mean generation to be conceived as a 'pervasive social cause that can have ramifications for many social phenomena'; rather, the Mannheimian historical, social generation is a 'dependent variable' for which a number of conceivable causes can exist. In his own theorization of how generations are formed, he pointed at a number of locations where such 'causes' might be found, the primary 'cause' (constitutive for generation formation) being a 'particular kind of identity of location' that members of a cohort share. The task of historical and sociological research is to discover, in each concrete case of generations ('dependent variable'), what are the particular socio-historical conditions ('independent variables') in which individuals become conscious of their common situation and make this consciousness the basis of their group solidarity (Mannheim 1952 [1928]: 290).

Mannheim's generation is also not a structure in the same sense as class (of the class analysis) is, and as also gender can be understood to be. Social structure is, of course, a central concept in sociology and there is a wide disagreement about what it can be made to refer to. For instance, Porpora (1998) examines four different conceptions of social structure prominent in the field: structure as a stable pattern of aggregate behaviour, as lawlike regularities, as collective rules and resources (cf. Giddens 1984), and finally as a system of relationships among social positions. It is this last one that we find in the kind of class analysis that Wright proposes.[10] Classes, patriarchies and racial modes of exclusion can all be viewed as systems of relationships among social positions and, as Porpora adds, also on the micro-level the structure of units such as the family can be viewed as a system of relationships, namely those linking the husband/father, wife/mother, and children, all of which are social positions (Porpora 1998: 343).

Thinking relationally – childhood studies

Here, although without naming the particular structure formed by relationships between parent/child positions, Porpora in fact presents a case of a generational structure (on one particular institutional site). Like social structures in general, the familial generational structure is a nexus of connections among (generational) positions, and causally affects the actions of the holders of those positions while in turn being causally affected by their action (ibid.: 345). In other terms, structural relations are *internal*, or *necessary* relations (see Sayer 1992: 88–92) in that one position (such as the parental position) cannot exist without the other (child) position; also what parenting is – that is, action in the position of a parent – is dependent on its relation to the action 'performed' in the child position, and a change in one part is tied to change in the other. Internally related phenomena, then, are strongly interdependent although, as Sayer notes (ibid.: 89–91), the relationship need not be, and often is not, symmetrical in both directions.

As noted earlier, also the Marxist concept of class is one that clearly hinges upon internal relations: capital necessarily presupposes wage labour, and outside this relationship, it is no longer capital (in the Marxist, analytical sense). In non-Marxist analyses and in popular discourses, however, classes (or, more often, strata) are mostly defined differently, in terms of shared attributes such as income, education and status, and the 'class structure' is constructed by 'classifying' individuals according to their correspondence to such criteria. The result is that the relations between such classes (that is, relationships among holders of 'class' positions) are external and contingent.

Connell (1987) in effect argues that gender structure (called also 'patriarchy' in some discourses) needs to be theorized in terms of *internal* relations. His terminology is somewhat different, and based on an examination of current frameworks for theorizing gender where he critically looks at 'categorical' theories of gender proposed in sociology (Connell 1987: 54–61). Analysis of gender relations based on 'categoricalism' starts by taking the gender categories – that is, those of men and women – for granted and then exploring the relationship between them; differences between theories appear in the accounts they give on this relationship and not in the starting point – which is categorical. These theories all follow – in Wright's terminology – the model of an independent variable discipline. In setting a simple line of demarcation between gender positions, they do not pay attention to the process of how the gender categories and relations between the categories are constituted in the first place and are subsequently reproduced or, as it may be, transformed. As a result of this, categorical theories are forced to treat gender in terms of internally undifferentiated, general categories, and in the end invite criticism of false universalism and even of falling back on biological thinking.

The same risk is evident also in those structural approaches to childhood that identify the social category of children mainly on the basis of chronological age; children (as also adults) become in effect a demographical age category, or in the more precise demographical terms, a birth cohort (or a set of them) of individuals. Through this translation of the 'generational' into the social construction of 'age', the analysis in fact moves into the generations and cohorts strand of generational analysis, while the alternative relational notion of generation suggests further possibilities for developing structural analysis.

Connell's route out of such impasses is to move away from categorical towards 'practice-based' theorizing; that is, to focus, not on external relations, but on internal relations in the constitution of gender categories. Such a focus means studying process: 'how gender relations are organized as a going concern' (ibid.: 63) Conceptualizing gender in terms of internal relations has implications also for the methodology to be applied in empirically researching gender structures: it too has to be consistently relational.

A relational conceptualization of childhood can be done in terms of both external and internal relations. When children are defined externally, the basis for defining category membership is some observable similarity or shared attribute, or sets of them, among individuals. In practice, age turns out to the most commonly used attribute. But whichever defining property is chosen to make the categorization, the relations among members of the child category as also those between members of the two categories of children and non-children remain external and contingent. The research practices of structural sociologies of childhood, as they have been proposed so far, clearly follow this categorical approach (see, for instance, Qvortrup 2000).

A different, and theoretically far more promising, conceptualization of generational structures becomes possible by choosing to focus on internal connections in children's relationships to the social world. Now the notion of a generational structure or order refers to a complex set of social processes through which people become (are constructed as) 'children' while other people become (are constructed as) 'adults' (see Alanen 1992; Honig 1999). 'Construction' involves agency (of children and adults); it is best understood as a practical and even material process, and needs to be studied as a practice or a set of practices. It is through such practices that the two generational categories of children and adults are recurrently produced and therefore they stand in relations of connection and interaction, of interdependence: neither of them can exist without the other, what each of them is (a child, an adult) is dependent on its relation to the other, and change in one is tied to change in the other.

A specific concern in exploring the generational structures within which childhood as a social position is daily produced and lived has to be on securing children's agency. In relational thinking, agency need not be restricted to the micro-constructionist understanding of being a social actor (as in sociologies of children). Rather, it is inherently linked to the 'powers' (or lack of them), of those positioned as children, to influence, organize, coordinate and control events taking place in their everyday worlds. In researching such positional 'powers', they are best approached as possibilities and limitations of action, 'determined' by the specific structures (regimes, orders) within which persons are positioned as children. Therefore, in order to detect the range and nature of the agency of concrete, living children, the exploration needs to be oriented towards identifying the generational structures from which children's powers (or lack of them) derive: the source of their agency in their capacity of children is to be found in the social organization of generational relations. This, finally, grounds the fundamental importance of 'generation' in our work to develop sociological understandings of childhood.

Notes

1 This sense of kinship relations is the one that particularly demographers wish to reserve for generation (e.g. Kertzer 1983).
2 E.g. Jaeger (1977), Matthes (1985), Attias-Donfut (1988), Pilcher (1994), Pilcher (1995), Becker (1997), Corsten (1999) and Turner (1999).
3 The bases of the two positions – class and generation – of course differ, and generation – as well as all the further historical and social formations growing out of shared generational positions – is ultimately seen to be based on the biological rhythm of birth and death (Mannheim 1952 [1928]: 290).
4 For criticisms directed at Mannheim's theory, among them the assumptions on youth and socialization on which he relies, see Pilcher (1995: 23–5).
5 These include particularly the conceptual and terminological distinctions between generation, cohort and (individual) age (e.g. Ryder 1965; Kertzer 1983, Becker 1992; Becker and Hermkens 1993).
6 In her book on age and generation in Britain, Pilcher (1995: 22–5) presents the similar 'cohorts and social generation theory' as 'one of the ways in which sociologists have tried to explain the social significance of age'. (The other four in her book are: the life course perspective, functionalist perspectives, political economy perspectives and interpretive perspectives; ibid.: 16–30). An abundant discussion on the concept of generation and generational issues has in recent years been going on also in German-language social science research (and public debate);

see e.g. Liebau and Wulf (1996), Ecarius (1998) and Honig (1999). For some of the causes for this 'renaissance' see Corsten (1999: 249–50).

7 A rare case of this is the German research on 'Children: War, Consumption and Crisis' (Preuss-Lausitz et al. 1983), by a group of thirteen researchers, who explore the shared experiences of three differing cohorts of children in Germany after the Second World War. The research was done before the emergence of the sociology of childhood and the authors identified their projects as sited in 'socialisation history'. This book can in fact be seen to pioneer the sociology of childhood in the German-language area.

8 Harriet Bradley, too, in her book subtitled 'Changing patterns of inequality' (Bradley 1996), sees age as the more important 'dimension of stratification' than generation, and accordingly devotes one full chapter to 'Age: the neglected dimension of stratification'. Within that chapter, generation is given two pages, mainly introducing Mannheim's work.

9 On discussions on this in e.g. disability studies, see the collection edited by Corker and French (1999).

10 Although also among symbolic interactionists and network theorists (Porpora 1998: 343).

3 Negotiating autonomy: childhoods in rural Bolivia

Samantha Punch

Introduction – negotiating autonomy

This chapter, based on my empirical study of children's lives in rural Bolivia, exemplifies ways in which children as active agents can negotiate relative autonomy within the structural constraints of childhood in relation to more powerful, adult, social actors (see Harden and Scott 1998). The structures of adult society limit children's opportunities for asserting their autonomy. Children live in a world in which the parameters tend to be set by adults, especially in relation to children's use of time and space (Ennew 1994). Therefore it is important to see how they negotiate their position within the constraints of that bounded world. It is necessary to explore children's competencies and strengths, as well as their constraints and limits, and their strategies for negotiating with adult society.

Adult–child relations are based on unequal power relations between the generations but should not be seen in terms of independence versus dependence. Elements of exchange in reciprocal relations between adults and children should be considered (Morrow 1994). Adults' and children's lives are inter-related at many different levels; adults are often not fully independent beings (Hockey and James 1993). It is too simplistic to use the notion of dependency, whether of children on adults, or adults on children, to explain the often complex nature of the adult–child relationship. This chapter argues that adult–child relations should be explained in terms of interdependencies which are negotiated and renegotiated over time and space, and need to be understood in relation to the particular social and cultural context.

Finch and Mason (1993) explored the processes of negotiation of family relationships in adult life in the UK. Although their research is not about young children, it shows how people *work out* responsibilities and commitments in the absence of clear rules about precisely who should do what for whom: 'Family responsibilities thus become a matter for negotiation between individuals and not just a matter of following normative rules' (Finch and Mason 1993: 12). In the majority world,[1] where many children work, some parents are economically dependent on their children's contribution (Boyden et al. 1998; Schildkrout 1981). For example, Boyden (1990) noted that in some countries children can be the main or sole income-earners in the household. It could be argued that in much of the majority world, children's economic contribution to the household means that family relations of interdependence tend to be stronger. The relationships of interdependence between children and adults, and between siblings, and how they manage the distribution of work for the household is largely ignored in the literature on the household division of labour. However, the notion of interdependence does not simply account for the exact ways in which responsibilities are met by individual household members. Thus, this chapter argues that even though the cultural expectation in rural Bolivia is that children should have a strong sense of responsibility and obligation to their family, the ways these are fulfilled in practice are negotiable.

Mayall (see Chapter 9) relates negotiation to structure and agency debates (Giddens 1979) where people struggle to gain a better deal in their relationships within different structures. She identifies the concept of a 'continuously re-negotiated contract as a feature of children's relationships with their parents', suggesting that 'children seek to acquire greater autonomy through resiting the boundaries, challenging parental edicts, seizing control' (Mayall, Chapter 9). I would add that children's negotiation of a relative autonomy also occurs in their relationships with other children, especially siblings, and not just with their parents. Such negotiation varies according to the extent of interdependence between children and adults, between siblings, and between children.

Adults' power over children is not absolute and is subject to resistance (Hockey and James 1993; Lukes 1986; Reynolds 1991; Waksler 1991a; Waksler 1996). Children renegotiate adult-imposed boundaries and assert their autonomy, which can include decision-making, gaining control over one's use of time and space, taking the initiative to do something and taking action to shape one's own life. Thus autonomy is partial and relative, as no one lives in a social vacuum, and the ways in which one uses time and space, or makes choices, take place within social contexts involving other people, both children and adults. Autonomy is related to issues of power and control which is why it has to be negotiated within social relationships, especially by children who are faced with unequal adult-child power relations.

Relatively few studies have focused on children's strategies of resisting adult power and control (Goddard and White 1982). Waksler's research in the US (1991b; 1996) indicated that children may lie, fake illness, have temper tantrums or act extra cute in order to cope with and control certain aspects of their lives. Reynolds' study of South African children (1991) referred to children's strategies of negotiating relationships in order to secure help for their future, and she also highlighted children's rebellion in defying adults' wishes, with reference to gambling, smoking and refusing to do certain tasks. However, it must also be recognised that children's reactions to adult power range 'from unquestioning acceptance to instances of resentful resistance' (Mayall, Chapter 9). Within the two extremes of compliance and rejection, children's strategies emerge as they manage their responses to adult control. Children may not be fully independent, but they negotiate a relative autonomy within the constraints which limit their choices.

This chapter begins by outlining the social and cultural context in which the study children live their childhoods in rural Bolivia. The division of labour and the nature of daily work in rural households are illustrated whilst highlighting the opportunities and constraints which shape children's everyday use of time and space within their community. The chapter then examines the ways in which children in rural Bolivia manage their unpaid work for their household by using a range of coping and avoidance strategies. Children's ability to negotiate and bargain with adults varies according to the extent to which adults depend on children in particular social, economic and cultural contexts. This chapter concludes by exploring household negotiations between children and parents, and between siblings, in relation to their household obligations and responsibilities.

Children in Churquiales

This chapter draws on my ethnographic study of children's daily lives in rural Bolivia which explored how children negotiate their autonomy within and between the four main arenas of their everyday lives at home, at work, at school and at play (Punch 1998; Punch 2000). The study took place in the community of Churquiales, in the Camacho Valley of Tarija, the southernmost region of Bolivia. I visited a sample of eighteen households regularly in order to conduct semi-participant observation and semi-structured and informal interviews with all the household members. At the community school, I carried out classroom observation mainly with the eldest thirty-seven school children aged between 8–14 years. I also used a variety of task-based techniques at the school which included: photographs (which the children themselves took), drawings, diaries and worksheets (see Punch 2001).

Churquiales has a population of 351 spread amongst fifty-eight households, with approximately four children on average per household. The community is 55 km from Tarija, the regional capital, a journey of about four hours on the local twice weekly bus. Most of the families own 2 or 3 hectares of land, which they mainly use to cultivate potatoes, maize and a selection of fruit and vegetables. They also tend to own a small number of pigs, goats and chickens, as well as a few cows. Most of their agricultural and livestock production is for family consumption, but any excess is sold in local and regional markets. The community has a small main square, where there are three small shops, a church, a medical post, a small concrete football pitch and the village primary school, and around the square there is a cluster of households. The other households are more dispersed throughout the valley, up to about an hour and a half's walk away from the village square.

Most of the children in Churquiales face the same broad constraints of relative poverty and geographical isolation. The opportunities for waged employment are limited, and schooling is available only for the first six years of primary education. The community is relatively isolated, having limited access to the mass media, as there is no electricity and no television, and communication networks are not extensive. The main form of transport is on foot and there are no cars. There are no push-chairs for young children, so they are tied by a shawl and carried on their mother's back. As soon as they can walk they are encouraged to get used to walking long distances and from as young as 3 years old they can be expected to walk several miles if necessary. Children cover a lot of ground every day as they walk between their home and school, go to the hillsides in search of animals or firewood, fetch water from the river and carry out regular errands for their parents to other households or to the shops in the community square. (See Chapter 7 for further discussion of children's necessary contribution to household work.)

Children spend most of their daily life outdoors, facilitated by the temperate climate. In contrast, the indoor space of their household is very limited, usually consisting of three mud huts with tiled roofs: a kitchen (cooking with firewood), a bedroom (where all the household members sleep together in three or four different beds, with sometimes two or three children to one bed) and a room to receive guests (and eat when it is raining). This contrasts with many children living in colder urban areas in the minority world where their use of outdoor space is restricted and controlled, and most of their time is spent inside the household.

The following diary extract indicates a typical routine and daily movement for 10 year old Maria in Churquiales:

> I got up at 5.30 in the morning and I went to get water from the river. Then I went to milk the goats. I brushed my hair and had my tea with bread. I changed my clothes and went to school. I read a book and afterwards we did language. We went out at breaktime and I played football with my friends. We came into the classroom and did more language. I went home and my mum gave me lunch. I went to get water and helped my mum make the tea. Then I went to bring in my cows and when I got back my mum gave me supper and I went to sleep at 9.00 at night.[2]
>
> (Maria, 10 years)

This extract describes a common school day: children get up early (usually between 5–6.00 a.m.), put on their old clothes, and do a few tasks, usually while their mother is making them breakfast (although some children make their own). Such tasks include fetching water and/or firewood, letting the animals out of their enclosures, feeding and/or milking them. They have breakfast, change into clean clothes for school, wash their faces, brush their hair and leave about 7.20 a.m., depending on how far they have to walk to arrive for 8.00 a.m. start. When they arrive home from school about 2.00 p.m., their mother or elder sibling has lunch waiting for them (soup and a main dish).

In the afternoon, their household jobs vary according to the season and particular needs of the time. Afternoon tasks may include: looking after and feeding animals, helping with agricultural tasks, fetching more water and firewood, looking after younger siblings, washing clothes, or preparing food. If there is spare time children play or do their school homework. At approximately 5.00 p.m. they have their tea, which is similar to breakfast: a hot drink and a small snack. Then the animals have to be brought in to the paddocks for the night. This may involve travelling quite long distances to round up goats, sheep and cows from the mountainside. Some of them may have wandered off and be difficult to find. Donkeys and horses also have to be brought in and tied up for the night. Pigs tend to be easier to manage as they do not usually roam far. Finally, at about 7–8.00 p.m. they have supper, which is one dish, such as a soup or a stew, and tends to be the remains of lunch. Children go to bed shortly after supper, usually between 8–9.00 p.m. Since it gets dark quite quickly at about 6.30 p.m., the rest of the day is spent with candlelight, doing kitchen tasks such as supper preparation, or washing up.

In order to provide for the family's subsistence requirements, the households in Churquiales have high labour requirements in three main areas of work: agriculture, animal-related work and domestic work. In the countryside many jobs have to be done everyday, such as caring for the animals, food preparation, and water and firewood collection. The household division of labour is divided according to sex, age, birth order and household composition (Punch 1999). Children are expected to contribute to the maintenance of their household from an early age. Once children are about 5 years old parental expectations of their household work roles increase, and children are required to take on work responsibilities at home. As they acquire skills and competence their active participation in the maintenance of the household rapidly increases.

Bolivian children in rural areas carry out many jobs without question or hesitation, often readily accepting a task and taking pride in their contribution to the household. In addition, some household tasks, such as daily water and firewood collection, are such a regular part of their daily routine that they accept responsibility without having to be told to do them. Water collection is a child-specific task, usually carried out by young children as it is a relatively 'easy' job which children as young as 3 or 4 years old can start doing. They may begin by only carrying very small quantities of water (in small jugs at first), but by the time they are 6 or 7 years old they can usually manage two 5-litre containers in one trip. Since children are assigned this job from a very early age and it has to be carried out at least once or twice everyday, children know there is no point in trying to avoid doing something which is very clearly their responsibility. I observed that children frequently accepted responsibility for such tasks and initiated action to fulfil them rather than merely responding to adults' demands. Their sense of satisfaction for self-initiated task-completion often appeared to be greater than when they were asked to do something.

So, children in rural Bolivia are not only expected to work and are given many responsibilities but they are also aware of the importance of their contribution and often fulfil their duties with pride. Parents encourage them to learn new skills by giving them opportunities to acquire competencies and be responsible. Parents do not expect to have to remind children constantly of their tasks and may threaten them with harsh physical punishment if their obligations are not completed. Children are encouraged to be independent: to get on with their jobs, to combine work and school, and to travel large distances within the community unaccompanied. In addition, children are also expected to maintain interdependent family relations by contributing to the survival of the household. Furthermore, parents teach their children to try to be relatively tough, for instance not to cry if they fall over and hurt themselves, not to sit on adults' laps or be carried on mothers' backs once they are over about 3 years old, and to be able to look after themselves and younger siblings when parents are away from the household.

Despite similar broad constraints and cultural expectations of children in the community of Churquiales, children in different households face distinct limitations, shaped by the household wealth and composition. Children in different households also have varying opportunities available to them according to parental attitudes towards discipline, work and school, which have been shaped by parents' own education and life experiences. Furthermore, within households, children do not necessarily all experience childhood in the same way, and such differences are a result of their age, sex, birth order and personal attributes. These factors combine to shape individual children's life experiences, and the opportunities and constraints with which they can negotiate. Within the restrictions which exist at a community, household and individual level, children negotiate ways to make the most of opportunities. They make choices within the limited range of possibilities available to them.

Within this social, economic, physical and cultural context, it is now interesting to explore the ways in which these Bolivian children actively negotiate the fulfilment of their work roles within rural households. Despite the threat of punishment if tasks are not completed, or the feelings of pride and responsibility gained when jobs are carried out, children find some of their work very tedious or arduous or would rather engage in their own pursuits than do all their household chores. Thus, I shall show that, although children in Churquiales work as well as go to school, they do not merely carry out all of their work willingly, quickly and in immediate response to parents' requests. Children also have their own agendas and preferences for their use of time and space. They also expect to be able to play and pursue their own pleasures, whilst sharing out tasks with all household members including parents and siblings. (See also Chapter 5 for children's negotiation of influence.)

Avoidance strategies

When I asked children in Churquiales whether they could refuse to do a particular job if told to by their parents, half the children said they could say no, and the other half said they were obliged to do the job (see Table 3.1).

Table 3.1 Children's avoidance and coping strategies

Child	Age	Avoid?	How?
Cira	9	yes	tell my sister to do it
Benita	10	yes	tell my sister to go and do it
Inés	11	yes	tell my siblings to help me, and Ernesto helps me
Rosalía	11	no	I have to do it, or sometimes my sister does it
Yolanda	11	no	no
Eduardo	11	yes	I have to do it
Alfredo	11	yes	I get my brother to do it, Sebastián
Luisa	12	yes	I send my brother and sister
Julio	12	no	I escape
Dionicio	12	yes	I want to learn other jobs
Rafael	12	yes	I have to do it because they tell me to, I can't say no
Delfín	12	no	I can't say no, I have to do it
Vicenta	13	no	get my brother and sister to help me
Santos	14	no	I can send my brothers
Sabina	14	no	if they tell me to do something, I have to do it

They explained various strategies they used to avoid doing an adult-imposed task which they did not want to carry out. The most popular strategy was to send a younger brother or sister to do the task for them. Parents agreed that elder siblings were allowed to tell younger siblings what to do, regardless of their sex, and elder siblings could also punish younger siblings if they mis-behaved. Sometimes younger children attempted to send an older sibling to do a job that had been assigned to them, but with a much lower likelihood of success.

Half the children who began by saying that they could not refuse to do a task, extended their answer, indicating that sometimes they too used a partic-ular strategy to avoid doing a job. The two main types of avoidance strategies which children use are delegation to a younger sibling and escape: 'I can't say no, I have to do it. Or I do it with José (elder sibling), or I tell Hugo (younger sibling) to do it and he goes'[3] (Delfín, 12 years). Sabina explains her strategy: 'If they tell me to do something, I have to do it. When they tell me to do a job I don't want to do, I go off and visit my Uncle Carlos'[4] (Sabina, 14 years).

Escape can take several forms, such as pretending not to hear and wander-ing off quickly before the request can be repeated, or pretending to go and do the job, but then just going somewhere else to play instead. Alternatively if children are really defiant, they may refuse outright, and go off somewhere without taking any notice, but then will have to face the consequences (usu-ally some form of punishment) on return. Parents recognise that their children do not always do as they are told: 'They go off and play, and then they don't do it sometimes.'[5] Some parents get stricter, threaten them with punishment, or shout at them to help 'persuade' them to do the job anyway.

Coping strategies

When children are unable to use an avoidance strategy, they resort to a coping strategy in order to make a job more acceptable in their own terms, thereby making a tedious or arduous task more tolerable or enjoyable. (See also Chapter 6 for discussion of time-shifting.) One such coping strategy is for children to make their feelings known and openly state their dissatisfaction. Most parents say that their children often complain about doing certain jobs: 'My children say: "I'm not going to do it," and then they do go and do it all the same.'[6] Some children seem to enjoy protesting, but often give in and carry out the task. Their slight triumph is the complaining before doing the job, to make sure that the other person is aware of the sacrifice they are making by doing it, or of the effort involved, or of the valuable time it is taking up. Children also make symbolic protests to ensure that their complaints are registered with the parent, in the hope that they will not be given further tasks to do.

A favourite strategy which children use when they do not want to do a job, but see little possibility of getting out of it, is to persuade a sibling to help them. Having company means the job is less boring and can be completed more quickly. Alternatively they may chat or play while doing the task and it may take longer to complete. It also gives the child added satisfaction that he/she is not the only one having to do something while his/her siblings are doing nothing. Combining a job with play not only makes a job more enjoyable, but can also be a useful strategy to prolong a particular task and therefore delay the next one. For example, 10 year old Sergio offers to cook pancakes because he enjoys eating them and spends plenty of time playing and making the dough into interesting animal shapes. His mother remarked how he tends to complain before doing a job and that he seems to enjoy moaning about his responsibilities: 'He likes to be begged to do things.'[7] She sees her children as being quite lazy, but does admit: 'When they want to do something, they do it well and quickly.'[8]

The likelihood of a child complying with parents' requests also depends on the child's personality. Some children are more obedient and willing to work than others. Others can be more argumentative and rebellious. Parents often differentiated between their children, some as keen workers and others as lazier. For example, Beatriz commented that one of her daughters 'complains a lot, she's very lazy and argumentative'.[9] Similarly, another mother explained: 'It also depends on whether the child is active when working, others are slower.'[10]

However, it also depends on whether the children really *want* to do something or not. For example, cleaning out and feeding the pigs is definitely not something that Sergio (10 years) enjoys doing, but another job, going on an errand to buy something from the local store in the main square, is a task he offers to do, before he is even asked. He knows that there he is likely to meet some friends and can stop to play marbles for a while before returning home. This coincides with Reynolds' (1991) findings that young people often use tasks to escape surveillance and meet friends.

Sometimes children deliberately take a long time to complete a task, or they stay and play for a while before going back to their household, because they know that if they rush back home the chances are they will be given something else to do. This strategy is especially easy to employ when they are sent to check up on animals, since they can pretend they had to spend time looking for an animal that had wandered off, when really they were playing. Parents are often aware of their children's strategies for combining work with play. Sergio's mother indicates that she knows that her son prolongs his return home on purpose: 'What takes Sergio a long time is in Churquiales (in the main square). He stays and plays, he doesn't rush to come back.'[11] In summary, the three main types of coping strategies which children use are to complain, to enlist the co-operation of siblings and to prolong tasks to delay or avoid another one.

Household negotiations

For children to be able to use coping and avoidance strategies successfully, they must be able to negotiate their position in the household. This section highlights some of the ways in which children in Churquiales can negotiate with parents and siblings in order to influence particular outcomes.

> Felicia said to her four children: 'Someone has to go and milk the goats. Who's going to go?' They all quickly responded 'Not me!' So she chose one of them: 'Marco, you go.'
> Marco (14 years) responded: 'No, I'm not going to go, because yesterday I helped grandfather sow.' The children argued amongst themselves until finally Dionicio (12 years) reluctantly went off. He complained more than usual that day, because the day before it had rained and the river was good for fishing. The siblings had been assembling their rods to go and fish. Dionicio went quickly up the hillside, milked the goats and ran back to join his brothers and sister.[12]

One very common result of a child being told to do a job that they really would rather not do, is a sibling argument and ensuing sibling or parent-child negotiation. For example, the appointed child suggests another should be told to do it, usually justifying why they themselves should not have to (because they are busy with something else, they are doing their homework, or most commonly 'I did it last time' or 'I've just done such and such so why doesn't so-and-so do something, why's it always me?'). This tends to provoke a sibling argument along the lines of 'But I did such and such' or 'But I did it yesterday, it's his/her turn' or 'But I always do it.' With this kind of back-and-forth argument, one of the parents, or an elder sibling, usually has to intervene with suggestions of more jobs in order to divide the tasks between them. Sometimes the siblings themselves negotiate the outcome, often settling for going together so that 'No-one gets out of it.' Children tend to have a strong sense of justice, wanting their siblings to fulfil their share of the household's responsibilities. This can be seen in 12 year old Luisa's question to her mother: 'Has Carlos (8 years) been to get water yet? I've already been twice.'[13]

The following conversation is an example of child-parent negotiation in a household where the mother and eldest daughter share many of the domestic duties, and frequently have to negotiate who will do what and when:

Marianela: I'm not going to go.
Dolores: Now you have to go. Can't you take my place for just one day?
Marianela: No, I can't.
Dolores: But I always do it during the week.[14]

This conversation took place on a Saturday and refers to whether mother or daughter will take Ambrosio, the household's father, his lunch, which involves a half an hour walk each way. Dolores, the mother, usually does it during the week when Marianela (10 years) is at school, so feels that Marianela could at least do it at weekends. She tries to reason with and persuade her daughter that it is only fair that she do it for once. Yet Marianela is adamant, she has no desire to make the trip. In the end, her mother gave in and agreed to go on the condition that Marianela looked after Marcelo, her 2 year old brother, and kept an eye on the animals. This example indicates how parents depend on their children to carry out certain tasks but they have to negotiate how they will be divided.

The following example illustrates another strategy children use: to try to negotiate doing a different sort of job. They may say it is too difficult, or merely that they do not want to do that, or may offer to do something else instead:

> Angélica (10 years) was looking after the pigs. Her mother said to her younger brother Simón (7 years):
> 'Go and take the donkeys to Uncle Serafin's house, or if not, Angélica should go.'
> 'Let her go,' said Simón.
> 'Okay,' said his mum, 'But then you'll have to go and look after the pigs, because that's what she's doing at the moment.'[15]

This strategy does not always work, it depends on the urgency of the job needing to be done and on the parent's willingness to change the job for another one (and either leave the job undone for the time being, do it themselves, or convince another child to do it instead).

Parents also used strategies to encourage their children to carry out household tasks. One particular strategy was to tell their children the tasks they themselves had to do at that moment, appealing to their sense of responsibility and justice so that the children also do their share. For example, when 12 year old Dionicio complained about being sent to a neighbour's house to borrow some cooking oil, his mother became quite annoyed: 'It's as if I were the only one responsible for making sure there is food to eat. You're not lazy to eat but you're too lazy to make sure there is some food'[16] (Felicia, parent). She persuaded her children to help by making them realise that she needed their help, she could not do the heavy workload alone.

Children's mechanisms for asserting their relative autonomy

As has been shown, children in rural Bolivia develop a variety of strategies to avoid or cope with doing tasks. They learn negotiation strategies from their parents, siblings and other children, as well as devising their own. James and Prout (1995) suggested that children learn about appropriate strategies or forms of agency to employ in different contexts and 'some children become highly skilled and flexible social actors while others are less skilled, less flexible' (1995: 91). The ways in which children respond to adult control over their lives varies in different contexts, in response to different individuals, and depending on the type and location of the task. Thus, children have a repertoire of strategies and the way they deploy them is opportunistic. Such strategies also vary, not according to sex, but according to the particular competencies, personality and birth order of individual children.

The Bolivian children's coping and avoidance strategies must be understood within this specific context: children are expected to work and are active contributors to the household from a very young age. Many of their strategies are facilitated by children's high level of mobility within their community, it is their extensive use of space away from adult surveillance that enables them to employ such coping mechanisms. Children's multiple strategies are not merely used in resistance to adults' power, but are part of a complex process in which they assert their agency, creating time and space for themselves despite restrictions from a variety of sources, including adults, other children and structural constraints.

Parents may or may not know about their children's strategies. Children may attempt to hide their actions from parents or they may react openly in front of them. Even when children try to conceal their ploys to avoid work, parents may be aware of such behaviour. Parents' reactions to children's strategies may also vary from acceptance and compliance to restriction and oppression. They may appeal to their children's sense of justice and responsibility; they may remind them that they know about their strategies and encourage them not to engage in them; or they may threaten to punish them. Some parents are stricter and more likely to enforce punishment, others may be more willing to turn a blind eye. Parents' reactions, like children's strategies, also vary depending on their present mood, the nature of the task and the particular circumstances at the time. Furthermore, it should not be forgotten that adults, like children, also operate with a particular set of structural constraints (Layder 1997).

Similarly, adults and children both negotiate what they do. Some tasks are more appealing than others for children just as they may be for adults. Certain household jobs are vital but others can more easily be postponed or delegated. However, because of unequal power relations children have less choice than adults, as they are more likely to receive a punishment. Adults have more power over children to delegate or delay tasks, but children also delegate to younger siblings and within their constraints they negotiate ways to avoid or alleviate boredom of tasks and obligations. The avoidance and coping strategies outlined here are not always appropriate, and sometimes they fail outright despite attempts at negotiation. Nevertheless, this chapter has indicated that children do not merely obey their parents passively or without question.

Household power relations consist of power not merely between adults and children, but also between children. For example, birth order and sibling composition not only affect the work which children do (Punch 1999), but also influence the strategies they employ and household power relations. Younger siblings are less likely to be able to delegate tasks, but can ensure that tasks are shared amongst the siblings. Middle siblings have a greater range of strategies to use since they can delegate, negotiate or carry out tasks with either younger or elder siblings. Power is ubiquitous and multi-dimensional, and should be seen as more complex than a one-way linear relationship of adult power over children (see also Lukes 1974).

This study of rural Bolivia shows that the transition from childhood to adulthood is not a simple linear progression from dependence and incompetence to independence and competence. This chapter has shown that children move in and out of relative independence and competence in relation to different people. It has argued that the notion of interdependence is a more appropriate way to understand relations between children and adults, and between children (see also Chapter 4).

Household relationships are constantly being worked out and renegotiated through sibling negotiation and parent-child negotiation. Households are neither totally consensual units nor are they entirely sites of conflict (Cheal 1989). Household relations include a mixture of co-operation and competition. On the one hand, households function as units of mutual support and solidarity, where moral obligations and expectations are fulfilled (Friedman 1984). On the other hand, these are the result of long-term relationships built up over time and are subject to negotiation, tension and conflict (Finch 1989; Finch and Mason 1993; Katz 1991). Intra-household relations are based on simultaneous relationships of dependence and independence. Individual household members are dependent on each other for different things at different times, yet they can also be independent individuals asserting a degree of autonomy, controlling their own use of time and space, and pursuing their own self interests. Children use their resourcefulness to stretch adult-imposed boundaries to limits more acceptable to themselves.

Family expectations and obligations mean that most children have a strong sense of responsibility towards family members. Their sense of justice means that they try to ensure that all family members share the duties and responsibilities necessary to maintain the household. Families negotiate their intra-household responsibilities according to the different constraints and opportunities which exist, including household wealth, household composition, birth order, sex and age of siblings, and personal preferences of individual members. Children are competent at negotiating their role within the household, despite their inferior position in relation to more powerful adults.

Negotiation may include reaching compromises or balancing different interests, such as individual preferences and household needs. It may be co-operative or may involve conflict and tension. However, this chapter has shown that the ways in which these children create their own use of time and space do not all involve struggle. Sometimes children initiate their active participation in society, thereby asserting their relative autonomy of their own accord rather than merely reacting to others or to situations. This may occur for example, when they take the initiative to fulfil their household responsibilities without being told to by their parents or siblings. Similarly, the children often accept being told to do things by their siblings or parents and do not attempt to assert their agency by offering any form of resistance. However, this should not be seen necessarily as passivity on their part, but can be quite the opposite. They may be making an autonomous decision to obey and contribute rather than resist. Since it has been shown in this chapter that children can resist, compromise and negotiate, they can equally choose to comply and accept. As we have seen, children in rural Bolivia are often proud of the contributions they make by participating actively in their household or community, and such contributions are sometimes the result of their own initiative. Therefore, it should be recognised that children, as competent social actors, may choose to respond to the requests or demands of others with a mixture of obedience, compliance, defiance and resistance. Equally they may act on their own initiative rather than just respond or comply.

Notes

1 Minority world refers to the 'first world' and majority world refers to the 'third world'. Present terms used to differentiate the economically richer and poorer regions of the world are either incorrect or have negative connotations for the poorer countries by emphasising what they lack (since they are developing, less developed, etc.). The terms minority and majority world are the only ones to shift the balance so that the richer countries are described in terms of what they lack (population and land mass) which causes the reader to reflect on the unequal relations between the two world areas.

2 *Me levanter a las 5.30 de la mañana y me ido a traer agua del rio y despues fue a sacar leche de los chivos y me peinado y tomado mi te con pan y me camviado de ropa y me ido a la escuela y hey leido un libro y despues amos echo las lenguage y salido a recreo y amos jugado la pelota con mis compañeras. Amos entrado al curso y hey echo mas lenguage y me venido a mi casa y mi mamá me a dado a almorsar y me ido a traer agua y hey ayudado a mi mamá a cer te y me ido a traer mis vacas y venido mi mamá me a dado a cenar y me ido a dormir a las 9 de la noche.* (Tuesday 15 October 1996)

Where quotations have been used from the children's diaries or worksheets, the original spelling has been left in order to capture the tone of the regional Spanish language.

3 *No puedo decir que no, tengo que hacer. O voy con José o a Hugo lo mando y él va.* (Delfín, 12 years, November 1996)

4 *Si me mandan a hacer, tengo que hacer. Cuando me manda acer un trabajo yo no quiero acer me voy a mi tio Carlos.* (Sabina, 14 years, November 1996)

5 *Se van a jugar y ya no hacen a veces.* (Nélida, parent, December 1996)

6 *Mis hijos dicen – yo no voy a hacer, después igualito van y lo hacen.* (Marcelina, parent, December 1996)

7 *Le gusta que lo ruegan para hacer las cosas.* (Primitiva, parent, 5 August 1996)

8 *Cuando quieren hacer, hacen bien y rápido.* (Primitiva, parent, 5 August 1996)

9 *Se queja mucho, es muy floja y malcriada.* (Beatriz, parent, 17 September 1996)

10 *También depende del chico que sea activo para trabajar, otros son más despacio.* (Felicia, parent, 17 May 1995)

11 *Lo que se demora el Sergio es en Churquiales. Se queda a jugar, no tiene apuro para venir.* (Primitiva, parent, 5 September 1996)

12 *Alguien tiene que ir a sacar leche de los chivos. Quién va a ir?*
Marco, anda vos. (Felicia, parent, 20 April 1995)
No, yo no voy a ir, porque ayer yo ayudé al abuelo a sembrar. (Marco, 14 years, 20 April 1995)

13 *Carlos ya ha ido a traer agua? Yo ya he ido dos viajes.* (Luisa, 9 years, 17 August 1996)

14 Marianela: *Yo no voy a ir.* Dolores: *Ya vos tienes que ir. Un dia-ito no me puedes reemplazar?* Marianela: *No puedo.* Dolores: *Pero yo toda una semana.* (19 August 1996)

15 *Anda llevar los burros donde tío Serafín, o si no que vaya la Angélica.*
Que vaya ella, dijo Simón.
Está bien, pero entonces vos tienes que ir a cuidar los cuchis porque ella está cuidandolos. (Beatriz's household, 19 October 1996)

16 *Es como si yo fuera la única responsable para ver que haya comida. No tienen flojera para comer pero tienen flojera para ver que haya comida.* (Felicia, parent, 6 September 1996)

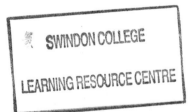

4 Dependent, independent and interdependent relations: children as members of the family household in West Berlin

Helga Zeiher

The introduction – the problem

Within families, children and adults continuously negotiate new relationships, and a principal focus for these negotiations is the division of domestic labour. Most investigations of this topic focus on children's emergence from dependence on parental care to independence (see, for example, Solberg 1990). However, the economic and social private household should also be understood as a unit of reciprocal care and interdependence (see Brannen 1995; Mayall 1998; Morrow 1996). This chapter explores ways in which families organise domestic labour within the constraints of their daily lives, and how dependence, independence and interdependence are intertwined in the child's relationships with other family members. The focus is on young schoolchildren. Which positions do parents assign to their children in the family household? How do children deal with the positions allocated to them? Which particular kinds of social childhood are produced by schoolchildren and their parents in the daily processes of dividing domestic labour?

Where parents in pre-modern households lived from the work of their hands, it was a matter of course that children would help out from an early age (see Chapters 3 and 7). The transformation to modern industrial society involved two strict divisions of labour with respect to children. Firstly, school work was differentiated from paid work, and modern childhood emerged as a social construct in its own right. Secondly, extra-familial paid work and domestic work were divided between men and women, and the pattern of the provider-housewife family emerged. In this pattern, women were responsible for ensuring the reproduction of society by means of their domestic work; rearing children as the next generation and providing for the daily regeneration of the masculine labour force (Rosenbaum 1982). The pre-modern principle that children's domestic labour was a matter of course, and something to be organised by parents, remained unchanged within this family pattern. It was up to the housewife to decide whether or not to delegate any domestic work to her children. These two divisions of labour, which were newly regulated in modern society, have continued to develop and change. Therefore, we must now ask which patterns of children's positions in the family household have emerged from recent changes in both the social construct of the learning child and the mother's position in the gendered division of labour.

The pattern of intergenerational labour division which is dominant in the social world of work – the separation of school work from paid work – was explicitly and purposefully designed and implemented by politicians and pedagogues, reaching children 'from the top down'. In the domestic world of work, however, the intergenerational division of labour is left to intrafamilial processes; it takes place at the 'bottom' – at the social base. Investigations must therefore start from the level of daily actions. In this chapter, I will take such a 'bottom-up' perspective and present case studies of three 10 year old children living in West Berlin to discuss some of the different positions which children can assume in the family household.

In order to reveal the kind of intergenerational relationships which are produced and practised in the daily lives of these children, it is necessary to be aware of the recent more general societal changes in such relationships. Therefore, let us first look at developments in the social situation of children and mothers in West Germany.

A child's position in the family division of labour is a result of covert and overt task-allocations, negotiations and struggles which take place within the asymmetrical power relationships between children and parents. As they grow older, children require less parental care and guidance. At the same time, they become more able to participate actively in domestic work. The course of this nature-based development is shaped by society; it can be either delayed or accelerated by societal concepts and structures of childhood. Child-parent discussions about the 'social age' at which a child is able, allowed or expected to perform a certain task reflect a double dynamic of time; the aging of the child on the one hand, and historical changes in attitudes to the course of child development on the other. Both children and adults carry society's patterns of childhood in their heads, though sometimes different interpretations of these.

In West Germany, a contradictory combination of delay and acceleration of social age has emerged in the final third of the twentieth century. This began in the late 1960s with a radical change in both methods of child-rearing and relationships between adults and children. The students of the 1968 movement called for 'anti-authoritarian' child-rearing practices, and met with a widespread response from educated young parents; children were to grow up free from domination. This coincided with a period of economic and political transformation. Technical progress and the expansion of the service sector created a greater demand for well-trained workers. The educational institutions were reformed and expanded. Education was democratised by opening up access ('education for everyone'), the standardisation of curricula and assessment, and an orientation to new scientific theories of human development, learning and socialisation. These theories focused on independence and autonomy as the most important aims of child-rearing, and on the child as a subject and actor in his or her development. Now, much more than before, the situation of children was marked by contradictions where their autonomy and dependence were concerned. On the one hand, children were accepted as subjects and actors earlier and more readily; on the other hand, they received more care and support from both private and public sources, and this dependence lasted for a longer period of time. On the one hand, the adult–child relationship was more equal; on the other hand, the structural control imposed on children by educational arrangements was greater. Educational scientists were highly committed to conveying their message to parents. Middle-class parents could be reached by public discussion; in some regions, universalist campaigns such as 'Letters to Parents' took place. These letters, containing age-specific advice, were sent to all parents free of charge at regular intervals from birth onwards. In fact, in the course of the 1970s and 1980s patriarchal dependency was replaced by a more equal adult–child relationship, if with certain social class differences (du Bois-Reymond 2000).

Let us now turn to mothers. In the provider-housewife family, household work was the mother's task and domain. In West Germany, this pattern has been preserved for longer than in many other European countries, and German family and school policies are still very much oriented to it (Pfau-Effinger 1993; 1996).[1] Almost all schools are open only in the mornings, mid-day meals are not provided; and institutional afternoon care is available for a mere 5 per cent of 6–10 year old children (BBWFT 1996: 38). In the first few grades, the school day is often very short and lessons begin and end at varying times on different days of the week.[2] This fits badly with the working hours of parents, who are forced to find their own ways of combining their professional situation with child-rearing and domestic work. Various types of individual solutions and many different time structures have thus emerged in family households (Diezinger and Rerrich 1998; Jurczyk and Rerrich 1993). Statistics on the paid employment of mothers show just how slowly the mother-as-housewife pattern is losing its significance. Since the 1970s, the percentage of West German mothers in paid employment has indeed risen, particularly where mothers of schoolchildren are concerned, but this increase is primarily in part-time work.[3] On the whole, today's West German mothers see the mother-as-housewife pattern positively, but only for a limited period and then often only for part of the time (Geissler and Öchsle 1996; Pfau-Effinger 1996). In contrast to the predominant ideas of gender equality, house-work is still largely the woman's domain (Koppetsch and Burkhart 1999; Meyer and Schulze 1994; Mischau, Blättel-Mink and Kramer 1998). (See Chapter 10 for a society where almost all parents work full-time.)

However, within this temporally limited continuation of the mother-as-housewife pattern, the relationship between domestic work and maternal duties has undergone a change since the 1970s. Under the influence of the women's movement, domestic work became unattractive in comparison to professional work (Pross 1975). The value of child-rearing, on the other hand, was increased in two respects. Firstly, many women began to see motherhood as a self-realisation project within an individualistic life plan. Women want both to provide their children with optimal care and to lead their own lives

(Rerrich 1983). Secondly, children began to receive more social recognition as a result of the reforms at the end of the 1960s and the rapid expansion of the educational system mentioned above. The main focus of maternal care shifted from the provision of practical domestic services and physical care to supplying the child with personal, emotional and cognitive stimulation, in addition to managing daily life and supporting the child's school career, leisure-time activities and friendships with peers. This, too, enhanced the status of the mother's role. Middle-class mothers, in particular, have since approached this kind of child-rearing in a semi-professional way, all the more so now in view of the bleak employment prospects for today's children (Pasquale 1998). Thus, for the last three decades, the developments in the social situation of children and of women in Germany have been interlinked.

The questions posed at the start of this paper are to be addressed against this multilayered background, thus providing them with a historical dimension.

Theoretical and empirical approach

A theory of children's social relationships in the family household

In order to investigate the child-adult relationships that occur in the process of dividing domestic labour, a conceptualisation of domestic labour focusing on social relationships between the generations is required. When the division of labour in families is regarded as gendered, as is usual in sociology, housework is likened to work in the labour force, and the unequal character, distribution, and value of housework are determined (e.g. Oakley 1974; Ostner 1978). This gender approach is not suitable for investigating the position of children in the family division of labour, however. A special generational approach must be used in order to take into account the peculiarity of the relationship between parents and non-adult children.

It proved helpful to look at the way Max Weber defined the social relationships of the private household, taking this peculiarity into consideration. Weber describes the mother-child relationship as 'a biologically based household unit that lasts until the child is able to search for a means of subsistence of his own' (mother-childcare community), and he defines the household as a 'unit of economic maintenance', that 'involves continuous and intensive social action' of all members (economic community). In the family, these kinds of social relationships are 'crossed' (Weber 1956: 276–7). Weber thus separates the asymmetrical parent-childcare relationship, the importance of which decreases over time, from the relationships emerging from the common life of all members of the family household which are, in principle, characterised by equality (if power differences are overlooked) and duration. This analytical separation makes it possible to study how the two are linked in particular cases.

Developing these Weberian definitions further from the point of view of children, I distinguish the following social forms of children's position in domestic labour. In the parent–childcare community, domestic work is done in order to fulfil the needs of the children:

- Parental childcare. Children are the object and recipient of services provided (primarily) by their parent(s). As the child grows older, the amount of this kind of work decreases. (Dependence)
- Self-care by the child. Children take an active part in meeting their own needs. As the child grows older, the amount of this kind of work increases. (Independence)

In the economic community, all work is geared towards physical needs and the social and emotional well-being of all members of the family:

- Domestic work for the common good. The child takes an active part in meeting the needs of the family as a whole. (Interdependence)
- Care for others. In the provision of reciprocal care, the child takes an active part in caring for other members of the household. (Reciprocity)

Hence, the research question can be reformulated as follows: How do children and parents, in the course of their particular daily lives, 'cross' these social forms of domestic work and thus dependent, independent and interdependent relationships?

The research approach: shaping daily life

Every family has a set of tasks which must be carried out in order to ensure the reproduction of the daily life of its members. Tasks recur at longer or shorter, regular or irregular intervals. The allocation of recurring tasks takes place against the background of a long-term regulation of responsibilities and duties. Family members negotiate who does what and when, thereby negotiating their dependency and power relationships. This often occurs implicitly. Decisions are negotiated for both long-term task assignments and duties, and for one-off activities. Although certain patterns remain constant, the division of labour in the family is an ongoing social process.

From the point of view of the child, these housework decisions are part of the continuing sequence of decisions by which their individual daily life is shaped. Over the course of the day, and having negotiated the constraints and opportunities prevailing at the time and place of each decision, children determine which activities they will perform. This process takes place in an environment which is made up not of an unrelated set of conditions or of the circumstances at a particular moment in time, but of a flow of events which extends throughout the course of the individual's life. This flow consists of a mixture of single and recurring events, with regularities related to times, locations and other social agents. A 'temporalised environment' in this sense is unique for the individual and dependent on the individual's choices over the course of time. Through this particular environment, societal processes and structures become relevant.

This concept forms the basis of a research design developed by Hartmut J. Zeiher and Helga Zeiher (1994).[4] The daily lives of a small number of 10 year olds from selected Berlin neighbourhoods were investigated in detail. Each child was followed through the entire sequence of their daily activities on seven days. During each day under investigation, the child kept a short record of each activity (type of activity, time, place, persons involved). The next day, the child was interviewed. Following the sequence of activities recorded in the interview, the child related how each activity came about, and described the circumstances and background of the activity, as well as its history in their life. This one-day-record, next-day-interview procedure was carried out seven times over a two week period, thus providing a record of roughly 150 activities per child in chronological sequence, along with the time, place and social circumstances in which each activity occurred. Further interviews were conducted with parents and with those employed in the institutional facilities provided for children in the urban setting.

The analysis of the material was broken down into the following three steps:

> First step: Reconstruction of decisions. Analysis began at the point of transition from one activity to the next. For each child, every single change of activity was analysed in order to find out how and why the new activity came about. The reconstruction of a decision of this kind is based on a psychological theory describing how particular actions are generated under a particular set of internal and external conditions. Such a theory and procedures for the analysis of the children's sequence of decisions have been developed by the authors.

> Second step: Case studies. The analysis of single decisions was the basis for subsequent work at the level of the individual child. Each of their decisions was considered, and used to derive the following characteristics for each child: the set of their intentions; the nature of their particular temporalised environment; and their action-generation system as a habitualised means of deciding what to do next over the course of the day, thus negotiating their intentions with prevailing environmental features. A case study was elaborated for each individual.

> Third step: Comparison of case studies. Comparisons were made in order to outline differences and similarities in individual childhoods, and to reveal general characteristics of social childhood which are apparent in the daily life of particular individuals.

The following case studies addressing the position of children in the division of domestic labour have been taken from this research project.[5]

Individual childhoods: case studies of 10 year old children

Thomas, Konstanze and Silke live in the western part of Berlin. They were chosen to be presented here because their mothers – each of them in the labour force – differ in their understanding and performance of household and mothering tasks. The aim here is to show how children achieve their personal position in the intergenerational relationship of the family household by shaping their activities in view of the demands, constraints and possibilities which they meet in the family.

Thomas

When Thomas' parents got married, Herr T. was employed in his father's small business and Frau T. was a sales assistant in a bakery. She gave up her job when Thomas was born, and remained a housewife for the next eight years. Herr T. then took over his father's business, and Frau T. also began working there for several hours a day. However, she alone remained responsible for child-rearing and for doing the housework for her husband and son in accordance with the gender division of labour in the provider-housewife-family pattern.

Frau T. sees it as her responsibility to create and maintain the prerequisites for a suitable childhood for Thomas, ensuring school attendance and opportunities for play. The family's daily routine is structured around regular waking and bedtimes, as well as breakfast, midday and evening meals together. The exact times are fitted around Thomas' school schedule. This is possible because the family business and the apartment are situated in the same building. Frau T. wakes Thomas in the morning. She sets the table before calling him for meals, lays out his clothes, and buys and wraps the gifts when he is invited to a friend's birthday party. In all of Frau T.'s actions, Thomas is given priority. Whenever he has questions about his homework, he phones his mother at work, and she then 'charges straight upstairs' to help him. Thomas has only two small domestic duties, both in his own interest. Once a week he must put away his toys so that Frau T. can clean his room; and he must also clean out his mouse cage every week; Frau T. is afraid of the mouse.

In this family, the parents have established a clear separation of the generations. The parents alone are responsible for and active in the common areas of family life; they alone ensure the reproduction of daily life, each within the confines of their gender role. The child is the recipient of care and services.

How does Thomas deal with this?

In the seven days under investigation, Thomas helps his mother with only one activity: When going to the library to borrow some books for himself, he also returns a book for his mother.

Thomas carries out his two weekly duties reluctantly, and never on his own initiative:

Monday, 1.10 p.m. in the living room after lunch with his parents: Thomas is free until 3.00 p.m. when he has arranged to meet his friend Hannes. He has no homework, and has only one chore before going out; Frau T. has asked him to tidy his room. Thomas does not feel like it; he thinks he still has plenty of time to do something else first, and decides to play with his cars. However, he does not play in his own room – presumably because that would remind him of the tidying he still has to do – but in the living room.

1.35 p.m.: A telephone call draws Thomas away from his cars: Peter has called to ask Thomas to go cycling. Thomas decides his prior arrangement is less important and rings Hannes to cancel it. Thomas now has to tidy his room in the half hour before Peter is due to arrive. As time is short, Frau T. helps him.

Through his slight reluctance – waiting to be told to do his chores and then putting them off to the last minute – Thomas demonstrates that this kind of work does not really fit into the family's generational system of labour division.

Thomas remains within this system in accepting the services provided by his mother, and even affects a generational separation of his own by cutting himself off from his parents whenever this is possible – both spatially and with respect to his activities:

Sunday, 12.13 p.m. back at home from a family cycling trip: Thomas has a lot of free time, firstly until Frau T. has prepared lunch, and then until about 3.00 p.m., when a trip to visit his grandmother is planned. Thomas retreats to the balcony, taking with him two things which separate him from his parents: an exciting book and his mouse. Even if this was not his conscious intent, the mouse – which is allowed to run about on the balcony – keeps his parents away. Not only does the balcony door have to stay shut, but Frau T. is afraid of the mouse.

Thomas leads his own life, parallel to that of his parents. His activity is concentrated in the area assigned to him; in his own room he occupies himself with his toys, books borrowed from the public library, music and television. Outside the apartment, his friends are of central importance. Both indoors and out, he has his own world, quite separate from that of his parents. Outside, he cultivates multiple interests and friendships in a responsible, enthusiastic and prudent manner. He is passive in the family world, but active in his own child's world.

Frau T. endeavours to surround Thomas with care and to keep him dependent on this. Thomas, by contrast, would like to lead his life independently. These are opposing forces. Thomas reacts to the comprehensive maternal care by distancing himself from his parents. He increasingly cuts off his child's world from the domain of his parents, and extends this sphere both spatially and temporally. Thomas is engaged in a continual struggle with his parents over how far away from home he may go, and how long he is allowed to stay away. He persistently oversteps the set boundaries, thus forcing his parents to adapt their concept of the child's 'social age' to his actions. For example, he is now allowed to stay at the playground with friends instead of going home immediately after school for lunch with his parents. Following an initial period of resistance, Frau T. now keeps Thomas' lunch warm if he does not turn up in time.

Thomas seeks independence and the opportunity for self-determined activity, and indeed finds these outside the family, with his peers. But he does not escape the protective sphere of the parental home by fleeing to the alternative protective sphere of institutional leisure activities organised and controlled by professional caretakers. Although he enjoys playing football, for example, he has categorically refused to join a football club. His counter-world to the childhood which has been constructed by adults consists only of children.

Konstanze

The K. family consists of Konstanze, her parents and 2 year old brother. From 8.00 a.m. to 4.00 p.m. on working days, a further eight young children are present in the family apartment, where Frau and Herr K. run a private day-care centre. The day-care business was established when Konstanze was six months old, enabling both parents to stay at home and look after her. Frau and Herr K. thus extended their parental care for Konstanze to providing care for other children, and now earn their living from this. While Konstanze grew out of the need for such intensive care, taking care of small children has remained a dominant feature of the household; on the institutional level with a constant supply of toddlers, and on the private level with Konstanze's little brother. Konstanze is no longer a member of the collective of young children, but this constitutes an integral part of her daily environment.

There is unquestionably a great deal of work involved in combining family life with running a childcare institution. Frau and Herr K. share this work, but Konstanze is not included. Only once in the seven days under investigation was Konstanze asked to tidy her room, and only once – when there was a lot happening at once – did Frau K. ask Konstanze to get the children out of bed after their midday nap. Konstanze's only duty for the common good of the household is taking out the rubbish, for which she earns pocket money. Occasionally, she likes to go and fetch bread rolls from the bakery in the mornings.

Frau and Herr K.'s commitment to ensuring optimal conditions for Konstanze was not restricted to her pre-school years. As she grew older, they modified and extended their care for Konstanze into the extrafamilial areas of life in which she became involved. Frau K. was active in the refurbishment of the neighbourhood playgrounds. She is parents' representative at Konstanze's school, and both parents help with school events and trips. They organise piano and ballet lessons for Konstanze, and take her there by car. Frau K. also looks after Konstanze's school friends, checking and helping them with their homework. Thus, Konstanze is set to remain in the position of a care-dependent child.

How does Konstanze deal with this?

> Thursday, 10.50 a.m., having come home from school unusually early: Konstanze finds small children all over the apartment, crawling around, playing or sleeping. Her parents are fully occupied with looking after them and preparing the midday meal. Nobody requires anything of her. Lunch will not be ready for two hours, her piano lesson is not for another two hours after that. The only thing she has to do is a little homework. Konstanze wanders around the apartment, drifting from room to room, not doing anything in particular. In the end she stays in the kitchen with her mother and brother and does her homework in five minutes.

> 11.10 a.m.: Again, Konstanze does not know what to do. She drifts aimlessly around the apartment, plays with the toddlers a little, but is later unable to say quite what she did: 'Something or other, well, this or that, nothing worth mentioning.'

> 11.30 a.m.: Frau K. decides to go and do some shopping. Konstanze wants to accompany her.

> 12.00 p.m., back home: 'I was here a bit, there a bit . . . and well . . . played with Lego for a bit.'

> 12.50 p.m.: The family has lunch. Afterwards, Konstanze has nothing to do while Frau and Herr K. clear up and get the toddlers ready for their afternoon nap.

In this sequence, the domestic environment is merely a backdrop for Konstanze's aimless actions. There is no interdependence of action between Konstanze and the social events in the household. She has neither the same needs as a small child, nor specific tasks of her own. She is accepted, but stands apart, the events having no specific connection to her as a person. She is associated spatially and temporally, but not through her actions. Drifting along in the external course of events, but not constituting a necessary part of them, Konstanze is very much left to her own devices. However, she remains dependent, as she does not know how to use this opportunity to realise her own goals independently or to assume a level of responsibility with regard to the day-care centre. She does not in fact steer her daily life.

When considering the reasons behind the lack of both independence and responsible cooperation displayed in Konstanze's behaviour, it is not so much the personality-related reasons which are of interest here, as the explanations rooted in the particular situation of this family. The extent of her parents' care is limited to improving Konstanze's social environment; at home, in the neighbourhood, at school. They place Konstanze at the centre of the environmental possibilities, but do not attempt to exert any direct influence on how she relates to these environments or how she leads her life within them. This gives Konstanze the freedom to arrange her time and actions. But during day-care hours, Konstanze is constantly attracted by opportunities for action, making it seem unnecessary for her to begin anything on her own initiative. In addition, the action model with which they set an example for Konstanze is reactive and not intrinsically goal-oriented; in caring for eight small children, Frau and Herr K. constantly have to react to unforeseen events. It should be added that Konstanze displays similar behaviour outside the family: she participates indiscriminately in all leisure activities on offer. Not once during the seven days investigated did Konstanze arrange to meet up with her friends on her own initiative. She dawdles around outside along streets and in playgrounds, waiting for an opportunity for action to arise from the environment.

Konstanze is an extreme example of a 10 year old whose position in the household remains almost exclusively on the passive side of the parent-childcare community. Because the parental care which she receives is overpowering, one-sided, and extends to all areas of daily life, Konstanze manages to make the transition neither to independence and autonomy, nor to the interdependence and reciprocity of the domestic 'economic community'.

Silke

Silke lives with her mother, who is a teacher, her stepfather, who works as a research assistant and is currently studying for an exam, and her 12 year old sister Nina.

From Monday to Friday, all family members get ready to leave at the same time, but independently of one another. There is no set morning schedule. The time from Silke's return from school at noon until the evening meal at around 6.30 p.m. is also characterised by independent activity by each family member. There are no regularities or requirements as to the midday meal. Between 1.00 p.m. and 3.00 p.m., those who are at home quickly prepare a simple hot meal. Silke sometimes eats lunch alone, sometimes she is joined by her sister or her parents. Each family member pursues their own interests until the evening, whether they are home together or not. This does not exclude the occasional common activity, for instance when Silke and her mother go shopping together. Nina is seldom at home in the afternoons. Twice a week, Frau S. does not come home from work until late afternoon. Herr S. is fairly flexible as to the time and location of his work. When Silke's parents are at home in the afternoons, they usually work at their desks. Although their doors are open, they are available only for short interactions. They do not wish to be disturbed, and do not usually intervene in the children's daily course of events.

The fact that Silke and Nina are left to themselves during the day is counterbalanced by the time Frau S. spends with them in the evening. She devotes her undivided attention to her career during the day, but to her daughters in the evenings. Then the course of events unfolds smoothly, without the need for set rituals, either in the kitchen while the mother prepares the evening meal, in the girls' bedroom or the living room. They tell each other about their day. Frau S. reads aloud from a book, asks about homework and sometimes helps Silke with her school work. She is also teaching Silke to play the flute. Mother and daughters often play games together, and sometimes go jogging. At some point in the evening, the whole family sits down to eat together; sometimes a full meal, sometimes just a light supper.

The division of domestic labour in this household is linked not only to this daily rhythm but also to a weekly rhythm of independent and common activities. The weekends consist entirely of group activities, although individuals may occasionally have their own plans. On Saturdays, the whole family cleans the apartment together.

Frau S. has given Silke and Nina joint responsibility for a number of household chores. It is up to them to tidy the room they share, look after their guinea pig and do two general household chores: emptying the dishwasher and taking out the rubbish. They are not only responsible for performing these recurring tasks – according to a prearranged weekly schedule which is hung on the pinboard – but also for ensuring the functional division of labour. If it is Nina's turn to empty the dishwasher but she goes out without doing it, then the responsibility is transferred to Silke. (That the girls do not always realise what has to be done early enough, meaning that their parents sometimes have to remind them, is another issue.) The weekly house cleaning is organised as a common undertaking by all family members. The sisters are responsible for their own room and, to this extent, only practise self-care. But in the temporal and social context of this general cleaning activity, the boundaries between work for oneself and work for the community dissolve. Frau S. says that Silke and Nina are 'actually drawn along by our activities'.

How does Silke deal with this form of organisation of the household community?

Silke looks after herself during the daytime, is competent and never bored. She has developed her own activities and interests, maintains close contact to her friends, and coordinates her personal needs with the opportunities presented by her environment.

Here, she has integrated her personal rhythm into the daily rhythm of the family as a whole:

> Tuesday, 12.55 p.m., returning from school to an empty apartment: Silke resumes an activity she was occupied with before school; sorting through some old photographs.

13.35 p.m.: Nina and Herr S. come home. All three go into the kitchen where they prepare and eat a snack. Silke tells her step-father and sister about a piece she is learning on the flute.

14.03 p.m.: Herr S., Nina and Silke go into the girls' room where Silke performs the flute piece.

14.14 p.m.: Herr S. starts work at his desk and Nina gets ready to go out. Silke starts her homework.

15.00 p.m.: Silke has now 45 minutes free before leaving for her art and craft course. She spends the time doing a jigsaw puzzle.

Silke tends to go home quickly after school, because she needs the peace and quiet, solitude and self-determination of an activity which has nothing to do with school. Only after such a period of calm does she feel able to start her homework, and only after this lunchtime break at home does she feel ready to go out and meet other children again.

This rhythm helps Silke to cope with her independence. It is an important prerequisite that she is able to embed the daytime phases – in which she makes her own arrangements and acts independently – into the overarching rhythm of family life. Silke is not released into a void within the family. The temporal limit of the phase of independence, and the certainty that a period of intensive maternal care will follow, create a protective sphere in which her independence is not overtaxed. The care relationship between Frau S. and Silke does not require her to be dependent, indeed, ways of gradually reducing this dependency are actively sought. Self-care does not take the place of parental care, however. Rather, both remain interlinked within a context of security and freedom.

Silke is well on the way to vacating the position of a recipient of services in the 'care community', not only by acting independently, but also by becoming a responsible member of the 'economic community'. Her parents, especially Frau S., retain responsibility for the functioning of the household as a whole. Accordingly, Silke explicitly justifies the domestic work she does, stating that her parents need help and that her mother has too little time or is too tired. This is her way of accepting the generational hierarchy of responsibility. At the same time, however, it changes the structure of this hierarchy. The care relationship is one-sided between parents and small children, but becomes reciprocal through mutual assistance when motivated in this manner; the daughter takes on responsibility for her mother.

The duties shared by Silke and Nina form another path to the interdependence of the 'economic community'. The two girls share their household chores equally. This area of domestic duties can be seen as a joint subhousehold. In as far as the duties are in the girls' own interest, Silke and Nina appear to be independent when the family household is regarded as a whole. Within the subhousehold, however, interdependence and reciprocal responsibility can be observed.

By what kind of intergenerational relationship is this family's daily routine determined? The founding principle of the division of time and labour here is equality of the genders and the generations. Silke, Nina, Frau and Herr S. are all involved in their own extra-familial work and activities during the working week. The parents' paid work, further education and sports activities are treated in the same way as the daughters' school work and child-specific recreational activities. This corresponds with the virtually equal responsibility accorded to all family members with regard to leisure-time decisions and household work. While the children are still young, however, small areas of life within which the girls' equality is yet to be realised remain distinct. Thus, Silke can develop independence and a sense of responsibility within a protective sphere and, at the same time, extend the scope of these from within, in as far as her own strengths and needs allow.

Ways out of dependency

Three case studies cannot represent the multitude of constellations to be found in reality, but each case investigated here is located at a different point in the field of reality. If we are to learn about intergenerational relationships in today's childhoods from these case studies, we must be aware of the positioning of each child in this field. In the following, I will try to place each of the three cases in a field which has been shaped by the historical trends described above. Thomas', Konstanze's and Silke's daily lives have been investigated at the same time. Yet, societal tendencies which emerged at different historical times affect their daily lives. Past cultural patterns are still present alongside recent ones, and in the lives of particular children, these fit together in different ways.

Thomas and Konstanze have very one-sided positions in the household: both are exclusively recipients of their parents' services, and do very little domestic work, either for self-care purposes or for the common good of the household. This is something they have in common with perhaps half of West German schoolchildren.[6] There seems to be a very strong tendency not to involve children in domestic work, thus establishing the household as a protective sphere from which all work, apart from school work, is excluded. The historical development by which children were removed from the world of work has now spread rather successfully to the private household. At the beginning of these processes, children were excluded from productive labour by the state enforcement of compulsory school attendance. Their exclusion from the domestic world of work occurred later; an inconspicuous development which took place in private homes and received little public attention. This development, too, was to the benefit of the children's school work.

Two historical periods in this development can be distinguished. In the first phase, children – especially boys – were cared for at home, so that they would be able to do school work outside the home. Thomas' mother can be classified as acting in ways typical of this phase. The women's movement has barely affected her at all. She embodies the mother-as-housewife pattern which was dominant in the middle of the twentieth century. Here, domestic work was subject to a clear gender division of a hierarchical order. Within the household, the wife acted as a servant for her husband and children. Children, however, were generally expected to 'help their mothers', and were thus at the lowest level of the hierarchy. The male-female division of paid work and housework was reproduced in a weakened form, with girls and boys being allocated different types of tasks and different amounts of work. Thomas no doubt benefits from the comprehensive services of his mother not least because of his gender. Frau T., however, justifies her actions in a way that is in keeping with current concepts of childhood, by saying that she is supporting Thomas' development. Yet both motives have the same outcome: Thomas is not expected to participate.

Thomas deals with the position his parents assign him by splitting his everyday life into two sections. One section consists of the protective sphere of childhood created for him by his parents. Here, he enjoys being waited on, and accepts the fact that his parents make the decisions, while he is dependent. However, he tries to suppress this section both spatially and temporally in order to make more room for the second section. This consists of a self-created child's world, completely independent from the adults'. With his friends, he leads a social life in which the children themselves actively produce a separation of generations.

It was characteristic for the first historical period that children could emerge from dependency only by escaping the hierarchical system, and separating themselves in their own autonomous world of play from the protective and educational sphere of childhood which the adults had established in the family and in the school. Children were entitled to do this; from the adults' point of view, this 'child's own world' symbolised the intended separation of children and was thus ideologically idealised (Honig 1996).

In the second period, beginning in the late 1960s, the social definition of what constitutes a child's education was extended from the confines of the school into play and leisure activities, as well as the family environment. All activities of daily life in which children engage were now defined as relevant for education and development. Every aspect of childhood was reflected upon and stage-managed. Children thus became more dependent on adults, but at the same time, they were entitled and indeed expected to act independently, and personal relations were less hierarchical. The separation of the generations appeared to undergo a subtle reversal. Parental care thus came to mean the comprehensive furthering of the child's development – to such an extent that children were not to be expected to do any work apart from this extended form of educational work.

The behaviour of Konstanze's parents is located at this point on the historical continuum. The reasons for Konstanze's release from domestic work lie in this understanding of parental care. Konstanze's parents have consciously accepted the high level of responsibility for child development ascribed to parents in the concept of socialisation popularised then. Both have little formal education, which perhaps explains why they have been less receptive to recent theories of personality development of the child, but are nevertheless very much aware of what is and can be done in the furnishing of children's environments. They have devoted themselves to providing Konstanze with everything that the social structures of childhood have to offer where education and leisure time are concerned. For Konstanze, the path to independence is blocked by the sheer extent of the care provided by her parents. Whatever she does outside the family household, her parents are also there, using their influence to ensure that both the circumstances and the people involved are favourably disposed to their daughter. Konstanze thus remains dependent in all domains. As shown above, this dependence extends deep into all of her actions.

Silke's mother also subscribes to this last view of parental care, but has interpreted it in quite a different way. Her intention is not so much to ensure that the environment is favourable for her child, but directly to support personal competencies. In her work as a teacher, she has come into direct contact with current concepts in education and developmental psychology. Practical services – like those performed by Thomas' mother – and organisational services – such as those rendered by Konstanze's parents – do not constitute a substantial part of Frau S.'s care for Silke. On the contrary, her support consists of emotional help towards self-help and the encouragement of independent action, even in the sphere of domestic labour. Hence, Silke's form of dependency is different from, but no less subtle than, that of Konstanze. Frau S. no doubt links the self-care tasks and domestic duties which she expects Silke to carry out to the pedagogical aim of enabling Silke to practise both independence and responsibility in the household. This corresponds to the widespread tendency of parents to see children's domestic labour (in as far as this is expected) as 'instructional rather than instrumental', its point being 'not to assist the mother, but to educate the child' (Zelizer 1985: 99).

Silke's domestic labour may indeed fit her mother's pedagogical concept, but it does not serve pedagogical purposes only. On the contrary, within the time structures of this household with two working parents, Silke's labour is essential. Silke does not need to look for independence outside the home, or to struggle for it within the family. In the daytime, her action space in the family household is not, in principle, any different from that of the adults. Like the other members of the family, she looks after herself to a great extent; she also organises her time herself. And like the adults, but to a lesser extent, she is responsible for certain chores that serve the common good, and organises the execution of these herself. Single tasks are not delegated to the children in a hierarchical approach. Rather, domestic work is divided into a series of juxtaposed areas for some of which one particular member of the family is responsible, while others are tackled by several family members in cooperation. This horizontal and, in principle, egalitarian division of labour enables Silke to be simultaneously independent and integrated into the family household.

Here, a potential change in the intergenerational division of domestic labour – a third phase in the historical development – can be seen to emerge. The 'parent-childcare community' comes to an end relatively early in some areas of life, because children have to look after themselves while parents are at work during the day. Thus, the generations are forced to become independent of each other earlier, and as a consequence of this, the 'social age' of the child may be redefined (see Solberg 1990). While the first and second periods of the intergenerational division of domestic labour were characterised by the construction of childhood as an educational period and by concepts of intensive mothering, impulses for further change can be expected primarily from another source: changes in the organisation of the private household. The fact that mothers are more frequently in paid work plays an important role here, but the restructuring of domestic labour due to developments in technology, service markets and lifestyles presumably does so as well (see Zeiher 2000).

Such developments could lead to a dissolution of the domestic community, each member of the family attending primarily to their own interests and needs. But Silke's case shows another possible direction of development: towards interdependence and reciprocity; a readiness to share responsibilities and cooperate for the common good, based on both the acceptance of principal equality between the generations and emotional affinity between child and parents.

Acknowledgement

The author gratefully acknowledges the work of Susannah Goss who translated the chapter from the German.

Notes

1 This is true for West Germany, but not for the former GDR. Here, state propaganda obliged children to help out at home and thus relieve their mothers of the double burden of both a family and full-time employment (Kirchhöfer 1998).
2 Out of consideration for working parents, there is now a move in some areas to keep children at school for the whole morning throughout the week.
3 In 1996, 15.7% of women with two children worked more than 36 hours a week, 11.2% between 21 and 35 hours, and 25.3% less than 20 hours a week. 3.1% were on maternity and child-rearing leave, 4.2% were registered unemployed, and 40.5% were not on the labour market (BFSFJ 1997: 109–23).
4 Several studies addressing specific sociological questions have already been conducted on the basis of this research design, in particular the project 'Places and Times of Children's Social Life' (Zeiher and Zeiher 1994).
5 op. cit.
6 No empirical studies have been conducted on the housework carried out by children in Germany. However, the results of several investigations into the activities which children focus on in their spare time lead us to conclude that about half of West German schoolchildren do very little or no work in the parental household (see Zeiher 2000).

5 The negotiation of influence: children's experience of parental educational practices in Geneva

Cléopâtre Montandon

Introduction

The study of childhood and children remained for a long time trapped, both conceptually and theoretically, in the prevailing sociological or psychological approaches of socialisation. Sociologists spent considerable energy studying adult-initiated processes supposed to transform children from a-social to social beings. Psychologists were absorbed in the study of the internalisation by children of social demands. Most socialisation research understood children as objects. Children were defined negatively, not according to what they are, but according to what they are to become (Alanen 1990; James and Prout 1990). Problems and issues in connection with children were most often examined through the lenses of this adult-centred approach to socialisation. Researchers analysed the influence of parents or the family on children (Peterson and Rollins 1987). They examined the effects of parental educational strategies on children's development, school performance or health, worked on the effects of the family structures and dynamics on what children became later in life; studied the impact on the parents and indirectly on the children of various intervening agents and institutions (Pourtois and Desmet 1989). Most often, however, researchers ignored how children themselves experienced these influences (for exceptions see Milkie, Simon and Powell 1997; Cullingford 1997).

This chapter is based on a research study which examined some aspects of children's experiences of their parents' educational practices (Montandon 1996, 1997). It presents the conceptual background of the study, followed by some research results and a discussion of various types of experience; it concludes with comments on the ways children manage and regulate the constraints and the influence of family settings.[1]

The study took place in Geneva, a cosmopolitan Swiss canton with a population approaching 400,000, a third belonging to various ethnic minority communities. Switzerland was one of the last countries to sign the United Nations Convention on the Rights of the Child (in 1997!). Having a federal political system, cantons have varying approaches to children, the family and schooling. Generally speaking, however, the responsibility for children's welfare rests mainly with the family (see Mayall Chapter 9 for the UK). There are few family policies and, in complement, government spending is the lowest in Europe. Things have started changing lately because economic conditions have become more difficult for raising children. Furthermore, divorce rates are quite high; 42 per cent of today's marriages will end in divorce, with higher proportions in the cities. Lone-parent families are rapidly increasing and new forms of poverty are emerging. The birth rate is around 1.5 children per woman, 1.28 for women of Swiss nationality. Though mothers are increasingly working outside the home, they still do more household chores than men (52 vs. 22 hours per week); girls help more than boys (13 vs. 8 hours per week). Children live in fast changing family environments and parents are less and less sure about their education and future.

In Geneva, compulsory education starts at 6 years, but from age 4 children can attend the 'école enfantine'. More than 90 per cent join the school system at this age, and slightly over a third of all younger children (0 to 4 years) go for part or the whole day to various day-care centres, kindergarten and similar institutions. According to the law, public primary schools are expected to complement family education and parents are supposed to support the school's mission. However, there is no consensus about what these terms mean. Teachers see their role as mainly academic and criticise parents for not giving 'good education' to their children, for not teaching them politeness, respect for others and relational norms. Parents expect teachers to participate in this trans-mission. These issues are present in the debates concerning the reforms being gradually introduced in the Genevan primary school system, which are based on child-centred principles. The academic effects of these reforms cannot be foreseen today.

What is certain, however, is that children's lives are increasingly controlled and institutionalised. Homework takes up part of their free time out of school and the child-centred reforms do not necessarily guarantee more autonomy. Though, for example, the reforms recommend the creation of class and school councils with pupil representatives, some children consider this procedure as imposed by adults. Furthermore, about one third of the children who go to public primary schools are enrolled in various extra-curricular activities organised by the school system: adult supervision after school for homework, but also at lunch-time or early in the morning. A galaxy of activities further organises the time of (mainly middle-class) chil-dren, such as music and other lessons and sports. Last but not least, an ideology of protection is gaining ground and one may expect further restrictions in children's freedom of movement in the future. It is therefore interesting to examine how children themselves in Geneva experience their socialisation environment.

Conceptual and methodological approach: in the steps of a sociology of childhood

Following the fast growing sociology of childhood, this chapter considers children as social actors participating in interactions, activities, exchanges, negotiations and adjustments which contribute to the construction, perpetuation and transformation of their social world. They are seen not as just playing the roles attributed to them but as producers of social processes as well as products. The theoretical approach presented in this chapter subscribes to a comprehensive, Weberian, view, attentive to the meaning children give to their experiences, the reasons they attribute to them (Waksler 1991c). Children are considered not as 'cultural dopes' but as knowledgeable members of their social world, being well aware of the various processes they are engaged in, and willing to discuss them if given the opportunity. This approach, however, does not ignore the fact that children's experiences do not occur in a social vacuum. It represents a combination of structural and interpretative perspectives in the field of the new sociology of childhood (James, Jenks and Prout 1998).

Experience is a central element of the research presented here, namely the experience children have of their socialisation, in the family and the school. It was conceptualised as comprising three interdependent dimensions, that is their representations, their emotions and their action in relation to adults' socialisation practices. This paper, however, focuses only on some aspects of their experience of family socialisation.

But what does the particular experience of socialisation consist of? How is one to approach it and what aspects of this socialisation should one cover? One way is to take into consideration the main social dimensions of school socialisation, expressed in the principal meanings attributed by society to schooling. Children build their experience of their own socialisation when facing these main goals, which can be seen as corresponding to three main rationales (see also Dubet 1991, 1994):

1   The *transmission* rationale has to do with the culture conveyed to children in the main educational settings. The agents involved in socialisation – parents, teachers and other adults – try to transmit the knowledge, the values, the ideals, the culture of their group.

2   The *organisation* rationale concerns the structures and methods encountered by children in the various educational settings. The socialisation process takes place in particular structures (more or less authoritarian, formal and so on), adults using specific methods and means; for example parent and teacher educational styles may differ.

3   The *orientation* rationale has to do with the projects the main socialisation agents have for the children as regards their school and work/career, their future. This is done in more or less constraining ways through the process of evaluation, selection, counselling, and children develop a rapport to this orientation.

Children's experience of family socialisation was thus conceptualised as consisting of their representations, emotions and actions as regards the transmission, organisation and orientation rationales developed in their families. Data were collected on the children's representations of what their parents transmitted to them, of the methods they used, of the projects they had for them; on the children's emotions as regards what their parents taught them, as regards parental authority and future plans; finally, on the children's actions in relation to what their parents transmitted to them, to the parental demands and authority, and to the plans they made for the future. It was hypothesised that the children's particular experiences at home represent distinct types of rapport to their family socialisation.

The three components of the children's experience and the three rationales of the socialisation process formed the backbone of a semi-structured interview guide, comprising general open-ended questions. The sixty-seven children who participated in the research came from four classrooms in the canton of Geneva, representing different social backgrounds. The thirty-five girls and thirty-two boys (aged 11–12 years) were interviewed twice, first at home and then at school. Each interview took between 60 and 90 minutes. The interviews were tape-recorded, transcribed, and two types of analysis were carried out: a content-analysis of all the transcriptions, which extracted the principal categories organising the children's experience and discourse, and an in-depth analysis of the interviews of twenty-four children, which disclosed four types of rapport to family socialisation.

The experience of family socialisation

This section presents some aspects of the threefold experience children have of their socialisation at home, in terms of transmission, organisation and orientation.

The children's experience of family transmission

Children have many ideas as regards our first dimension of the educational process, namely the transmission of the family heritage. Almost all children have a clear idea of what they expect from their parents. Most express needs which are probably fulfilled in reality, others formulate their expectations indirectly – for example asking that their parents cease treating them as babies – and others wish for a number of things they don't get from their parents. Table 5.1 shows the principal types of expectations mentioned spontaneously by the children.

It is love, support, listening, understanding, comforting, all laced with humour, that children expect from their parents above all. 'I expect affection,' says a girl. 'They must take care of me and not only of their work. They must also stay at home a little bit. And also that they have understanding: we are still children, we can't understand everything, everything they say.' The same type

Table 5.1 Children's expectations of their parents

To support them emotionally	57%
To give them a 'good education'	30%
To stimulate their autonomy	24%
To guide them	19%
To help them with school work	13%
To provide material support	12%
To teach them things	6%

of discourse comes from a boy. 'I expect affection, love, and also niceness (gentillesse) and time. Parents play a big role for us.' One girl among many emphasises the need for support. 'I expect them to be here for me when there are problems, to try to solve the problem. Also try to be here, to give love, to be with me a lot.' Emotional and affective support expectations seem by far the most important.

From their parents children expect what some formulate as 'a good education', that is that their parents introduce them to the principles of good behaviour, so that other people will say, 'This child is well-educated.' They want their parents to teach them how to avoid doing stupid things. 'They must give me a good education so that I don't do stupid things when I'm grown up.' Reprimanding is considered part of this process. 'They must tell me if I do something wrong. They must reprimand me and tell me that I shouldn't do this or that.'

In a similar vein children expect concrete advice and guidance. They want parents to teach them how to control themselves, and how to get along in everyday life. 'When I don't know that I can't do certain things, well they should explain to me.'

However, many children expect their parents to stimulate their autonomy: 'They must give me a good education, not spoil me too much (me chouchouter); not do too many things for me, so that I start getting along by myself.' A girl adds: 'because when I'm grown up, it's not my parents who will take care of me, I will have to take care of me myself.'

Some children wish their parents to give them support for their schoolwork. 'They must help me with my homework, when I don't understand; but when it has to do with French they can't' (this being an immigrant family). Other children mention they expect material support, to be fed, to have a roof, means of transportation and money. 'I expect love, tenderness, and enough money so that I can live well. Not too much, because then I would be a spoilt child and I would make fun of the others who don't have much money.' As can be seen in this last quotation, children's accounts mostly combine expectations of different kinds, affective, material, educational and so on.

Sometimes their discourse seems contradictory at first sight. They wish their parents to help them and at the same time to avoid interfering. In fact they don't want their parents' solicitude to work against their own desire for independence:

My parents aren't really interested in my problems, well my father; my mother is interested a little bit. Parents must, I think they must be interested in their children and their problems. But my father lets me manage my problems alone. I think this quite good. I don't want my parents to help me deal with my problems, I must deal with them alone, I must learn to manage them because when I'm grown up, my parents will not manage my problems for me.

The image of the family which emerges from the children's accounts consists of a place where they expect security and emotional support. But if the children's affective expectations occupy a prominent position, the more traditional dimensions are far from absent. When their demands for a good education, guidance, school and material support are combined, they exceed the affective ones.

Children are very coherent in their expectations. When asked to say specifically what they wish their parents to teach them, a third mention interactional and relational norms: politeness, savoir-faire. They wish their parents to transmit values and qualities like love, listening to others, honesty. 'I want them to teach me how to listen to others, how to understand others, how to explain other people's points of view, this is crucial . . . [pause] . . . love.'

Many children wish to learn self-regulation. In other words they expect their parents to teach them how to control themselves, how to control their desires, including how to avoid spending their money all at once. They want to be taught how 'to be normal'. A boy said: 'They should teach me that we can't do whatever comes to our mind. Not spend the money we have. My parents tell me "You shouldn't get into drugs" and all that. I find it is good that they say that.'

Parents are also supposed to teach how to prepare for adult life. Some children think about their future job. 'Well, they should tell me what job (metier) would be good for me, whether I will enjoy such a job.' Encouragement of autonomy is part of this preparation: 'I expect them to teach me how to get along in life, so that I don't always go to them, ask them to lend me money and all that, that they teach me how to be responsible.' Girls more than boys want to be prepared for their future family. 'Me, I expect them to teach me about life for later on. For example, if I marry, I must know how to cook, how to do a whole lot of things.'

A few children think their parents should give them the keys to understand the world and how society functions. 'Well, awareness, since we don't learn that at school, awareness of the world, how to react, what to do. At school there is not much awareness, there is mainly learning.' At a more prosaic level, some expect to get practical knowledge: how to cook, how to drive a car, how to iron, and so on.

As we have seen, children expect their parents to teach them different types of knowledge: moral, practical, relational. They seem aware of their moral status (see Mayall Chapter 9). In fact, they put more emphasis on the acquisition of moral and relational competence than their parents do. The latter seem more preoccupied by the management of everyday life, by school requirements (Kellerhals and Montandon 1991). One can see that, on the relational level, what parents supply doesn't exactly correspond to what their offspring demand.

The children's experience of parental organisation of their socialisation

How do the children evaluate the way their parents organise the socialisation process in the family? Let us see what they have to say as regards parental educational practices, more particularly as regards parental authority, methods, punishments and supervision (encadrement).

Parental authority

Their relationships with parents is a subject children have a lot to say about. About one third of them describe themselves as good, willing (serviables), nice (sympa), polite, in other words as conforming. One girl explains: 'In fact I am always very nice. For example, when they scold and shout at me or things like that, I try to explain to them, I don't get annoyed, I don't go and sulk in a corner. In a sense I try to understand why she said that, why she scolded me, and then I give her my opinion on what she did. I'm not a girl who will bang the door of my room straightaway.' This apparently conforming behaviour by some children is not necessarily a sign of passivity: 'I conform because they are also my parents, they must be respected, because they also respect us. Sometimes I don't agree with them. (Pause) Yes, I don't agree, and then sometimes I shout because they don't understand. So that they may understand my reasons!'

Two-fifths of the children appear to be sometimes good and sometimes impertinent, willing and disobedient, pleasant and sulky, depending on their mood. They are variably conforming, depending on the days and the situations. 'Well, I'm sometimes very complicated (laughs). Yes, I irritate my mother and my little sister a lot. Sometimes, not always! And sometimes I help her a lot and my mother tells me sometimes that she is very happy to have two nice big girls, because we help her with many things.' In the same vein: 'When I'm in a good mood I'm not very agitated (turbulente), that is I go to my room and get on with my own things. When I'm in a bad mood, well when I get up on the wrong side, I do stir things up, I do anything, I can't keep still, I go to the garden, I come back, I play with my cat, I never stay put and then I'm always getting at (engueuler) someone.'

The children whom one may describe as rebels are a minority. They say they oppose their parents, that they are troublesome and ready to fight (emmerdeurs et bagarreurs), easily lose their temper, shout above other people, answer their parents rudely, don't do what they are asked. One boy said: 'If they ask me to go to the garage to fetch a bottle of wine or water, or something like that, I refuse.' A girl declared: 'I answer back a lot, I'm difficult as we say, that's what my parents say. I can see they get mad.' And another one: 'I harass them (emmerdeuse)! That means that sometimes I irritate my parents. I'm bad-tempered with them (hargneuse) . . . sometimes I say bad things, but sometimes it's not my fault.' This leads to fisticuffs (empoignades). 'Well, sometimes I'm bad, because they annoy me. Sometimes they hit me, like that, and then I hit them back.'

Parental educational methods from the children's point of view

In order to get the children's viewpoints on their parents' methods and authority some questions were presented to them about familiar situations. For example, 'What do you do when your parents: a) don't let you dress the way you want; b) don't let you go out with your friends Saturday afternoon; c) don't let you watch the tv programme you want; d) don't give you the money for you to buy something you want?'

The children's accounts display a range of reactions to parental authority and show many interesting elements as regards their relations with parents and their strategies (see also Chapter 3). A first reaction, quite frequent, is to submit without any discussion. One might characterise this behaviour as *conformity*; but it may be a strategy, depending on the child's evaluation of its advantages or the importance of the issue. As a girl said, referring to the situation where parents will not let her go out with her friends: 'Well, I obey, because I would be punished even more if they see that I go out secretly. So I prefer to obey.' A boy, who is under strong control at home, says: 'I give up, because if I insist talking about it, then it's likely I get punished, so . . . About clothes I do what they tell me, I can't do anything else.'

Another quite common strategy is the *circumventing of parental dictates*. Children find other means to obtain what they want. They save up to buy the desired object or ask their grand-parents to give it them; they get a friend to make a video copy of the film censored by their parents or they hide behind a piece of furniture to see the film. 'If I really want to see a film they don't want me to watch, than I do some zapping, leaving it the longest possible on the film I want to see.' When they are not given the money to buy something they turn to their friends for a little help: 'Well if I have some pocket money I buy, but otherwise I ask my friends to lend me some money, or I ask my brother, or things like that.'

The strategy of *wearing down* parental resistance is also quite common. Children repeat their demands insistently until they succeed, their parents yielding out of weariness. 'I keep on asking, I wear them out, perhaps they'll give way, but if they don't then I have to obey,' admits a boy. A girl gives a similar analysis. 'I have this method of getting them to say yes: I insist, I insist and I insist . . . And then, in the end, they say OK. Well, it doesn't work every single time, but when they're in a good mood, it works!'

Many children use the *vociferous defeat* strategy. They comply with what is asked of them but with overt demonstrations of their frustration: they cry, scream, bang doors, lock themselves up in their rooms to sulk and so on. They don't easily admit defeat: 'Well, when I'm irritated, I bang the doors and then I go and argue with them.' A girl only partly accepts defeat: 'I go to my room, I bang the door. I lie on my bed and read and I try to forget and tell myself, "It's always the same thing with my parents". And sometimes this makes me so mad that I throw my erasers all over the place. Then I go to my mother and say, "Explain this to me!"'

Some children choose *negotiation*. They agree to submit if their parents can prove their demands are well-founded; they do not obey without clearly understanding their parents' requirements. They are sensitive to the family situation and problems: 'I try to understand why they don't want me to go out and if they don't because of some family reason, then I give up on seeing my friends and I stay home. And if the reason is money I try to talk with them.' So children understand their parents' worries. 'I try to convince them to start with and if they say it's no, because of their responsibility, etcetera, if something happens to me, etcetera, I understand, they are worried about me, I understand.'

But negotiation is not enough for some children; they appeal then to *argument*. They engage in long discussions with their parents to show they are right. If this doesn't work then they ignore their parents' wishes. A boy whose parents wanted to interfere with the way he dressed but provided no valid arguments says: 'I reject their answer, I tell them that when they were young they wore these wide trousers (des pattes d'éléphant) too. If they continue to refuse, then as soon as I get out of the house I take my shirt out of my trousers.' A girl tries to show she is reasonable and claims her rights to go out: 'I try nevertheless to convince them. If for example we have no plans I try to tell them, "I also have the right to go out, I am big enough".'

Still other strategies are used by the children but less frequently. *Bargaining* is one example, when they agree to render a service to their parents in exchange for permission to go out. 'I do a chore at home and she lets me go sometimes.' A few children resort to the technique of *substitution;* if one activity is refused they console themselves by choosing another; if they are not allowed to go out, they watch a video, if they cannot see a particular film, they listen to music. Some count on the strategy of the *fait accompli*. When they feel their request will be rejected, particularly in matters of clothing, they do what they want without asking for permission, even if this means they will be reprimanded later. One boy mentioned employing a kind of 'terrorism', that is he attacks his parents when they refuse something: 'I shout at them, that they are rotten, not nice, that they have no heart, I sulk, I become bad, I pester them and sometimes I hit them a little, I push them; one time I pushed my mother against a cupboard, I gave her fright!'

Generally speaking the children are aware of their inferior position vis-à-vis the adults and adopt strategies corresponding to the power asymmetry. In situations where parents ask for a service, most obey. But this submission is not blind; the children have their reasons. Some obey because they don't want to be rebuked or punished. 'I don't want to, but my father scolds me, and in any case I have to do what he asks,' or 'If I don't do this job, well, my father hits me. I don't know, but I'm quite afraid when I'm scolded.' Others do as their parents say because they think parents do many things for them and so they owe services in return. 'I obey because my parents are nice with us. They give us whatever they can.' In some families it is the custom to render mutual services. 'At first I don't feel like obeying, but in the end I agree, because everybody has to take part in doing chores in the family, and I don't see why I should be the only one not to.' Some children refer to their status. 'I have to do what they ask, because they are my parents, I have to obey them.' Some think there may be a reward. 'I get angry and tell them that I don't want to go (on that errand). But in general I go even if I'm angry. Normally when I do a job they give me a toy.' One gets the impression that some obey because this allows them, in turn, to give their parents a lesson. 'Sometimes they tell me, "You go and fetch this in the kitchen", and then I stamp my feet, I show I'm irritated and then I push my chair around loudly – sometimes it falls over, and well then I go to the kitchen, I bang the drawers . . . Sometimes I want to say why is it always the children who have to do jobs and not the parents, it's not fair. It's what I often tell myself.'

A minority however find a way to disobey. Some know how to stall, knowing that if they wait long enough, somebody else, usually the mother, will do the work they are supposed to do. 'I say I will do what they ask and then I don't. And sometimes I get told off a bit and I have to do it and sometimes the moment passes (ça passe entre les gouttes) and I don't do it.' Others evaluate the task and don't do it if it bothers them. 'If it's, for example, to sweep the kitchen, I don't feel like doing it and I don't do it.' Another trick for disobeying consists of delegating, preferably to a younger sibling, but also to an adult. 'If they ask me to go to the garage to fetch a bottle of wine or water, I refuse. I ask my father to go or my sister. But I fix it so that I don't go.' Finally, some children know how to dramatise, they threaten they will leave home, they lock themselves in their room, or they just show they are above the requests of their parents. 'I say "I'm leaving" (je me casse de cette maison) and then I take my things and leave. Well, I pretend, I take an empty suitcase, I leave and then come back . . .,' or another example, 'I say no and then I lock myself in my room. Actually I get bored in my room, I take something to eat and then I stay there till next day. I love this, because I have the TV, the radio, also the computer. And anyway my parents can't come in, it's locked.'

All these examples show that children can activate many resources in opposition to their parents, even though most of the time they feel obliged to obey. They don't always regard themselves as defeated, they consider themselves as full actors, claiming to be heard, asserting their desires and sometimes their rights. Their accounts show that many of them admit the legitimacy of parents' demands only if they are well-founded. They ask for a kind of authority which grants a large place to dialogue, to negotiation. In this they are children of modernity.

If most of these children say they are surrounded by parental care, and if a few seem being cared for, many are more critical. Some indeed emphasise the fact their parents are interested in them, understand them, advise them, console them, reassure them and intervene if necessary. 'They are interested, they listen to me, they try to solve different problems with me, they try to understand why.' However, for the majority of the children the parental interest and support is not so great. Some think their parents are mainly preoccupied with homework, or support them only with what they consider important: 'They don't meddle too much in my affairs with my friends, they say that it's up to me to solve them. They are rather interested in my problems at school.' Some children say the focus of their parents' interest misses the target and even that it is intrusive. 'My mother, if I have a problem with my boyfriends, she comes and says, "Oh, what happened, you must tell me, you must not have secrets from me" and I don't want to tell her, I have my secrets and that's all! I have the impression I'm a baby for them.' Finally, and rarely, some children feel their parents are not interested. 'We don't talk . . . and they don't care at all. They don't pay much attention to my life.'

All these children's accounts of their experiences of parental socialisation practices suggest that though children expect affection and support, guidance and security from their parents, they also fight for their autonomy. However, in their daily lives they feel more supervised than surrounded with care, more controlled than listened to. One observes a difference between their expectations and reality and they oftentimes voluntarily accept beings cogs in social processes of which they are well aware. As their accounts show, children are influenced by a social context which is in turn affected by them,.

Children's experience of orientation influences

The children in this study were on the threshold of important decisions as regards their school career. It is interesting to explore their experience of these decisions, which depend mainly on their teachers' evaluations but partly on the wishes of the children and their parents. Most of the children claim the freedom to decide. Many parents make them understand that at school they work for themselves and that it's up to them to choose their future. 'My mother tells me it's up to me. That she is not the one who will decide everything in my life. Well, I wouldn't want this to be the case.' If some children want to protect their freedom of choice, this doesn't seem to annoy all the parents. Some are happy to be thus discharged of this responsibility. Others don't have the competence to direct their child, as in the case of immigrant parents, who don't know the school system well enough. But if this makes things easier for the children who want to make their own choices, others have to fight to impose their ideas. Whatever the situation, however, a quarter of them know that their school career doesn't depend on their parents' wishes or theirs, for it is their school results which will determine their future. Many know already that certain doors are closed for them.

It is clear that parents generally influence choice of future jobs and professions. A small minority say their parents will not influence their choice and they seem very determined. 'It's not what they want, it's me who decides. It's me that said since I was little that I wanted to be a doctor, and I stick to this idea.' Some children, however, say that they don't know their parents' opinion on this subject, either because they never discuss this matter, or because their parents don't seem to be interested at present. 'I don't know what my parents think. I think they want to let me choose, they don't want to say "Yes, later on you will be a baker", it's not they who will choose my job.' The children's accounts indicate that about half of the parents try to influence their child according to their knowledge of her or his personality and abilities. Some parents try to awaken their child's ambition. 'They want me to have a good job, to continue my studies. Because my parents only went to primary school in Portugal and they don't want me to do the same.' Others state specifically what job their child should do later on, but some are quite discreet and a few do not interfere at all. 'They don't care whether I become a doctor or a road sweeper, they want my job to please me.'

Mostly, parents exercise influence on their children's choices. The children are well aware of their parents' wishes, and if some have internalised these and other constraints, they have not done so blindly.

Children's perspectives on their own status

How do children experience their own status as children? What do they say about their actual condition? Do they rejoice in growing up? Two-fifths say they look forward to becoming adults, a similar proportion show ambivalence, and the rest indicate fear of growing up. In the children's eyes the most positive characteristics of adult life are freedom and self-realisation: freedom to do things and decide by oneself, to be able to engage in activities reserved to adults, also to own certain things just for oneself, not to be obliged to share with siblings. Self-realisation contains many dimensions, physical, relational, professional and social. Many children look forward to exercising the job or profession they have chosen, others to having their own family. Still others aspire to being adults and be respected.

The children who are ambivalent talk about the constraints and difficulties associated with adult life. They are discouraged by the stress they observe in their parents, the heavy responsibilities and duties, the conflicts, fights, separations. To this they add physical problems: backache due to hard work and fatigue, pains during menstruation or childbirth. The children's accounts show that many of them consider their childhood as the time of privilege.

Expressing themselves about adult life is a way of expressing their perspectives about the status of children. Thus a child appears as dependent on others as regards freedom of action and financial autonomy. Children see that young age implies a lack of maturity, since many activities are forbidden. Respect is missing, since the status of being socialised carries a connotation of inferiority. One can understand why some children look forward to having an adult professional and family position. On the other hand, childhood offers some real advantages: being fed, having few worries or financial constraints, having the time to play, to 'hang out' (musarder), without being too much preoccupied with the next day.

Types of *rapport* to parental socialisation

Four types of rapport to parental socialisation emerged from the analysis of the children's experience (representations, emotions and actions) as regards the rationales of their family education. Of course, this typology is valid only for the present. Children may change the type of rapport to their parents as time passes. Like all typologies it is reductive and represents a tentative way of synthesising children's experience of family socialisation.

Temporary dependence

The largest group of children have this type of rapport with their parents. They belong to all social backgrounds, with a slight over-representation of lower-middle-class and working-class children. These children attach great importance to love and affection in family relations but what they mostly expect from their parents is a 'good education' and guidance, that is how to behave well: eat properly, be polite and orderly, how to deal with everyday problems, how to avoid drugs, how to avoid getting into trouble when they grow up.

As to the everyday organisation of their educational experience, these children are relatively quiet and obedient, rarely enter into disputes and accept quite easily that they should help at home, many of them thinking this is fair. Most of these children describe relations in the family as dense and warm.

Although they think they have a lot to learn from adults and do not fight against the limits imposed by their parents, these children say that they suffer from a certain lack of freedom and find adult control too heavy. This is why they are looking forward to becoming adults, so as to be able to decide by themselves and do what they want. For them, authority is a necessary evil associated with childhood, useful provided it is limited in time.

Their future orientation varies according to their social milieu. The good students belonging to high-status families seem ready to think that what matters for the future is to be able to express oneself, to be happy and motivated, to develop one's talents. The children belonging to lower-class families react in a more utilitarian way: what is important is to work at school so as to be able to find a good job and achieve higher status than their parents.

Escape in the family cocoon

This is the second largest group and includes children from a range of social backgrounds. They expect support and affection from their parents; they want to be helped and understood and to be protected. To a lesser degree they want their parents to teach them practical things and to give them a 'good education'.

Quiet and rather dependent, they feel much more comfortable at home than at school, love to feel their parents around, get bored or feel insecure when they are not there. They are afraid of losing their parents' affection if they don't behave properly or are more independent. They are surrounded by their family and at the same time controlled and relatively little stimulated to gain autonomy.

This important affective dependence leads to a tendency to conform to the desires of their parents. They don't try to refute what their parents say, being afraid to hurt their feelings. Generally speaking they accept control because, they say, this brings security and they need a frame. The children in this group do not rejoice in becoming adults because grown-ups seem to them to be under stress, to suffer too many constraints and carry too heavy responsibilities.

These children rarely have future plans. None seems to have a clear idea what their parents wish for their future. It is as if the family kept silent concerning the future of the child. One wonders whether it is the lack of parental encouragement as regards their autonomy that makes these children dependent and uninterested in their future, or if this is due to the fact that their parents – realising that their child has a relatively vulnerable personality – concentrate on offering security for the present and make no particular plans for the future.

Expressive negotiation

The children of this type, the third largest group, are good students and come from rather well-off families. From their parents they expect love, support, understanding and to be taught how to be nice, how to be attentive to others, how to make friends, how to show solidarity; parents should answer their questions about work and society. But they also seek self-expression and self-assertion and want their parents to show them how to manage by themselves, and to let them make their own experiences instead of protecting them or doing things for them; they like to be encouraged to develop their own tastes, talents, personality. In general, these children are stimulated in their family and are engaged in various extra-curricular activities.

The orientation these children experience relates to self-expression. The parents do not insist on the necessity of earning a living but on the importance of engaging in something which encourages the development of their child's personality and individual abilities. In these families it is stressed that it is more important to be happy than to earn a lot of money, although this does not prevent the parents from discretely encouraging their children's professional ambitions. Though the parents seem to let their children choose what they want to do in the future, they guide them to select among the various professions they consider favourable for their future career.

The relations these children have with parents are symmetrical. They simultaneously give affection and ask for affection. They communicate a lot with parents, talk with them about life in school, are not afraid of claiming their rights. When facing authority, they produce their arguments, sometimes contest the adults' opinions, conform if this is reasonable. They accept authority inasmuch as they are able to negotiate it and they all look forward to growing up.

Rebellion

A small number of girls fall into this group. What they expect from their parents has something to do with their social origin: transmission of norms and practical knowledge in working-class and immigrant homes; encouragement of autonomy and understanding in middle-class homes. These children do not formulate precise expectations of their parents. They are vague about their future and their orientations and tend to be more expressively oriented in the middle class, more utilitarian in the working class.

But what distinguishes most this group of girls is the organisation of family life. They show a certain distance vis-à-vis their parents and a great intolerance towards authority. Although they love their parents, communication seems impeded, fear or conflict are often present. These girls talk very little to parents about life in school, almost never about their feelings. They do not like parents to interfere in their life and they interpret parental questions as a kind of intrusion rather than as a sign of affection. They feel more comfortable away from their parents, do not seek their company.

At home they consider they are too much under control and they cannot stand parental authority. They often obey out of fear of being scolded, some of them try to fight back, to rebel, to manifest their discontent and disagreement. They find that being a child is not an enviable situation, because adults do not listen to them, do not trust them, treat them like 'babies', as if they didn't count. They look forward to becoming adults, in order to be respected at last, to be listened to, to have their ideas recognised and to have responsibilities given to them.

Some concluding remarks

No doubt it is still quite difficult for people generally, as it is for some researchers, to recognise what children say as worthwhile. Adults are suspicious about the authenticity or value of children's discourse and accounts, in spite of increasing numbers of studies in all fields which identify competence in very young children (Youniss 1980; Matthews 1994; Dunn 1988). The 'underdevelopment' of children is therefore no longer a valid argument for not taking into consideration their point of view.

The children's discourse presented in this chapter shows that they know how to express their relational experiences. Their accounts manifest their conception of their relations with their parents as regards the transmission of knowledge and know-how, which is inherited from the past; they show their experience of parental authority and demands, which has to do with their present lives; and they show their way of dealing with the future, as they react to the projects and plans their parents have for them. Through this triple reality they make sense of their socialisation and build their social identity in the process of co-constructing their relations with their parents. These processes do not lead to permanent constructions: the remodelling of relations is continuous, as they meet with new knowledge, interact with other socialising agents and institutions, confront new projects. Children change and they know it. Dependent children can become autonomous, rebellious children can develop empathy towards their parents. The children took part in the study at a specific point in their history and they gave examples of previous change, examples of the incessant interplay between what educators try to eradicate and what they themselves retain in order to construct their own trajectory. They did not give the impression of being trapped in a weighty and determinative habitus and their perspectives as regards their family context – and their school situation – show that they have introspective competencies and a critical spirit.

No doubt the transformations of contemporary society have exercised an influence on the principal dimensions of child–parent relations. Whilst in the past the various elements constituting parental education of children were articulated in a more or less coherent way, nowadays they are more scattered. In the past, for example, the transmission of family values took place within agreed parameters, children generally obeying parental authority, accepting the transmitted values, internalising the places assigned to them. Nowadays, family values reflect the pluralism of modern societies, the organisation of their transmission is more often negotiated between parents and children and the orientation parents would anticipate for their children has become more dependent on chance. We saw that children participate in an active, reflexive way towards the definition of their relations with their parents. Their experience is influenced by the latest transformations of our societies. It becomes necessary to question the dominant perspective as regards the children of Western societies, which, in the name of their protection as well as in the name of expertise concerning their interests, considers them as vulnerable and ignorant beings without taking into account the intrinsic value of their multiple experiences.

Note

1 The terms socialisation and education are used almost interchangeably. Both are considered here as processes of interaction, education being more specific and intentional.

6 What are schools for? The temporal experience of children's learning in Northern England

Pia Christensen and Allison James

Introduction

> 'It's just non-stop working and you're just going like this' (She sighs deeply) '. . . . and just writing everyday and it just gets real boring and sometimes you think, God, can't we have a week off or something? Cos it just gets really tiring . . . . . . Sometimes, when it's boring it just feels as though the day's never gonna end'.

This is the graphic account 10 year old Charlotte gave of her experience of everyday time at school during our recent ethnographic study.[1] Her words captured, very strikingly, the commonly expressed opinion that 'school is boring'. Drawing on accounts of the daily unfolding of child-adult relations at school this chapter explores why children may indeed describe their experiences of time at school as boring and it further discusses the implications this has for children's learning. The children's accounts of school as boring were remarkable for the very matter-of-factness with which they presented this view. It was often said in a repetitive, routine, manner which suggested that boredom was simply taken for granted. Although we are in no doubt that children also enjoyed the time they spent at school, the continual repetition of the notion that school is boring deserves explication. We framed our analysis of children's accounts of time at school, therefore, by asking the simple question, What is school for?, a question central for the project of schooling in which children and adults are engaged.[2] In this chapter we focus on how this project is accomplished at school by teachers and children, through an analysis of their accounts and of observations of everyday encounters and interactions in the classroom.

We draw particular attention here to the centrality of time and the temporal processes of schooling in child-adult relations, reflecting contemporary concerns about the context of children's learning experiences. Owing to changes in English educational policy including the introduction of a National Curriculum in schools, time has become increasingly a scarce resource at school, leading to concerns over the way time is allocated for different aspects of learning and the conditions and prospects for children's cultural development (Pollard 1996; Pollard et al. 1994; Carvel 1999; Almond 1999). In this chapter we reveal the critical importance for both children and teachers of control over time-use in relation to the social organisation and experience of schooling. Children's schooling takes place both in time and over time. It is predicated on a particular view of time passing in relation to broader perceptions of children's developing cognitive and physical skills and social competences which are played out through the highly routinised rhythm and pace of children's learning during the school day. As this chapter will show, this has particular implications for children's say over the way they spend their time and for their experience and understanding of school as part of their personal life project.

Ethnographic accounts of children's school experiences

Studies of children's school experience – their everyday lives in the classroom, relationships with teachers and with their peers – have constituted a large body of research within the sociology of education since the 1970s. Usually, though not solely, carried out using ethnographic methods, such work provided case-studies of children's school lives, revealing children as active participants in and contributors to the process of their own schooling. Classic studies of older pupils, Corrigan (1979) for example, showed how schooling can be experienced as an alienating system and demonstrated how pupils can circumvent the control structures of the school and learn to make the best of the bad job they consider schools to be (see also Willis 1977; Woods 1979). Studies of younger pupils similarly adopted a pupil perspective and explored children as social actors in the school setting. Pollard (1985), for example, demonstrated the different perspectives and attitudes which different groups of same-aged children held about their school experience and the strategies they employed in classrooms to negotiate it with their teachers and their peers (see also Sluckin 1981; Davies 1982; Sherman 1996).

Such studies, as Shilling (1992) notes, contrast strongly with another tradition within the sociology of education, which, also since the 1970s, has adopted a broad macro perspective and carried out structural analyses of the process and systems of schooling. Notable among this body of work is, for example, Bernstein's (1971) account of the classification and framing of educational knowledge, whereby he demonstrated the structural inequalities in access to knowledge experienced by working-class children; similarly, Bourdieu (1971) explores the ways in which, within the French educational system, the valuation of particular kinds of knowledges reproduces patterns of social exclusion. As Shilling argues, such approaches seek to explore 'the determining power of discourses and texts in "post-industrial", "information" societies which structure both consciousness and action behind people's backs' (1992: 72). This work tends to play down the agency of both teachers and pupils within the context of the school, a perspective which, as shown above, is paramount in ethnographies of schooling. These two research traditions,

Shilling (1992) argues, have created a micro-macro division which is in need of remedy. Drawing on Giddens' structuration theory, he suggests understanding schools as emergent and emerging institutions, as in process rather than as fixed sites of constraint; and understanding children and adults as having certain rules and resources which they employ and produce in their everyday interactions and negotiations. Reproduced, over time, these become sedimented as the institution which is called 'school', but 'school' is always nonetheless contingent upon the everyday decisions and actions of children and their teachers. In this sense the school is not fixed and given as a structured system but consists of 'reproduced relationships between individuals and/or collectivities across space and through time' (Giddens 1981: 169).

In this chapter we address some of these interactional processes involved in the project of schooling, by revealing ways in which the 'time of childhood' both defines and is defined by 'time in childhood' (James and Prout 1997: 231); that is to say, we show that children's school experiences are shaped by the temporal processes and practices through which their everyday interactions with adults and indeed other children unfold. By asking the question 'What is school for?' we argue that time figures as a key resource in and a structuring principle of practices at school and that the differential power over time which children and adults have influences children's experiences at school.

Our conversations with teachers and children revealed the conventional distinction between 'teaching' (teachers) and 'learning' (children). As twin aspects of the schooling process, this distinction signified the rather different approaches taken by teachers compared to children, perspectives, which, as we shall show, were articulated and concretised in the everyday temporal practices to be found in and across the different sites of the school and which were central to children's experiences of schooling. Unsurprisingly, and in line with studies of older children (Corrigan 1979; Willis 1977), we found that children and teachers do not necessarily agree on the educational project in which they are engaged. Sometimes their views of its purposes were shared, when, for example, the teacher and the children in the classroom worked effectively together; at other times their perspectives were incompatible; or they might indeed be in direct opposition.[3] In this chapter, then, we want to suggest that due attention has to be paid to the processes by which children's and teachers' perspectives and positions in relation to the educational project at school are both brought together and kept apart. Through this we can gain a clearer understanding of what school is for.

The study

We carried out our ethnographic study following groups of children during their last year at primary school (Year 6) and into their first year at secondary school (Year 7). This chapter is based on data produced while the children were at the three primary schools. The children lived in an inner city area of a large town and in a rural area in the North of England and the fieldwork was carried out by the authors, one working in each local site. The primary schools included a small village school of about sixty-five pupils and two schools each with about 225 pupils, one in the centre of the town and the other in a village. The study used a wide range of methods, such as individual and group interviews with children and their teachers, together with ethnographic participant observation of everyday life at school. In addition to these more conventional research techniques we developed a set of participatory research tools to explore children's conceptions and everyday practices at home and at school (Christensen and James 2000). In this way we gained a broad understanding of how children spend their everyday time and the meaning of school time for children.

School is for the future: teachers' views

In Year 6, both children's and teachers' work throughout the year is focused on the SATS tests[4] which take place during a week in May. We found that the expectation for children to do well at these tests was a central concern shared by teachers, parents and the children themselves, and indeed put much pressure on teachers, but especially on the children, whose good performance is regarded as of crucial importance. Their performance not only indicates how well individuals are doing and may determine how the secondary school views these new entrants to Year 7; it is also important in terms of the school's standing within the local community. However there were marked differences in the orientation of teachers and children towards the 'future' which the passing of these tests is held to represent, differences which are embedded in the distinction between the perspective of 'teaching' and that of 'learning'. The teachers' broad belief in the overarching purposes and value of primary school education for children's future was at odds with the practical task of teaching children on a daily basis within what they saw as an increasingly restrictive and regulated environment (see also Pollard 1996; Carvel 1999; Almond 1999). As one teacher saw it, ideally primary education was about creating opportunities for children through an early exposure to a wealth of different experiences:

> One of the things primary schools are always very good at, getting children involved . . . just opening up avenues for them for later life, involvement in as many things as possible which they may then pick up at secondary school and clubs at the weekends. . . . I have pupils who come back to me after years, who've said, 'Thanks for introducing me to table tennis because I've gone and enjoyed that activity over the years'. That's very rewarding and quite often they've forgotten the Maths lesson or the English lesson but they've remembered the (drama) production, the trip or the sport.

However, while stressing that in his view this was a 'very, very important aspect of primary education', he acknowledged that this broader educational goal was now increasingly at risk, owing to what he described as 'the press of standards, standards, standards' – that is, the necessity for schools to work towards obtaining the educational targets set out for them within the framework of the National Curriculum. In all three schools the teachers were, therefore, pre-occupied with how best to utilise the time and space available to teach differently abled children in the same classroom in order to maximise their ability to achieve these targets; the teachers drew on well developed practices and skills to provide this 'differentiated' education for children. Helen, a supply teacher, describes how she managed during one term to teach a Year 6 class whom she did not know, through spatially organising children in relation to time:

> There's information given to you of the ability range of the whole class and then I grouped . . . into six groups, six groups and on occasion they were working in six totally different groups, on occasion there might have been two groups working on the same level but they were working at different levels, so that I could stretch the more able, but also look after the low achievers, erm, but it's just basically, erm, experience of children, you know you only have to be with them for a very short period of time to realise what their actual ability is.

But children were not only grouped in accordance with teachers' judgments and evaluation of their academic abilities. In addition, some teachers also operated a system whereby different groups of children were seated either close to or distant from the teacher so that maximum attention could be given most effectively to those who were thought to need it most. In sum, therefore, the narrow, but very practical, objective of achieving particular literacy and numeracy standards for all pupils within a specified period of time has to override the broader aim of providing a rounded education for the person that the child is and will become. The latter simply takes up too much of the teacher's time as one head teacher noted: 'Many schools have ditched (extra-curricular activities) simply because they can't find the time . . . .'

Thus, in this study the schools which continued to try to set aside time for activities such as sport, music and drama, other than those scheduled within the National Curriculum, found that these had, increasingly, to be compressed into children's and adults' free time – play-time, lunch-time or after school. Following an OFSTED school inspection[5] in which criticism had been received concerning the amount of teaching time children received, one school decided to increase the school day by ten minutes to ensure that broader educational goals would not have to be sacrificed:

> We actually extended the length of the school day because staff felt that they wanted lunch time to do their clubs and they wanted the afternoon

play-time because they felt that children were then ready to do work in the fourth session of the afternoon, whereas without an afternoon play-time they would feel that the fourth session of the afternoon was very much a baby-minding session because the children weren't up to work.

However, although schools endeavoured to retain a commitment to such broad educational goals, in practice this was increasingly difficult to sustain. For example, the setting of yearly targets for pupil achievement by the government had meant, in addition to a narrowing of the curriculum, a change in the ways in which learning takes place. In one teacher's view the emphasis on testing and standards has meant 'that you are increasingly teaching more and more and more for children to jump through narrow hoops . . .', as Ms Smith, a Year 6 teacher, remarked. 'You find yourself teaching for the SATS . . . it's a way of teaching them how to get good marks.'

This emphasis on standards and testing she saw as leading to a deterioration in child–adult relations at school:

> . . . the rapport in schools sometimes goes down because teachers perpet-
> ually feel under pressure to perform to these results and that has an effect
> on the way that they conduct their lessons . . . there isn't scope any more
> for sort of saying, 'That's a great point, let's investigate that', picking up
> things that the children initiate and actually running with them.

As a consequence of these pressures, then, the project of schooling becomes increasingly under the teacher's, rather than the child's, power and authority, as one headmaster described:

> You'll start a lesson and you'll find that the children's interest is leading
> you towards a certain path and it's not in your plan. In the past you'd have
> gone down that path because the children were interested. Nowadays
> you're very much a case of 'This isn't in my plan and I didn't intend this
> to happen, stop it and let's get back on track.'

The time pressures brought to bear upon the structure of the school day mean, therefore, that the teachers did not often pursue broader educational objectives in their lessons and could only rarely make gestures towards the perspectives of learning which dominated the children's accounts of schooling, such as their central concern with friendship at school, their seating places in the classroom and the suitability of partners allocated to them for doing collaborative work. Instead, the teachers' concern was to get the teaching done well and efficiently. Time for them was a key resource. The following sections explore how children themselves experienced this disjuncture between the broad and narrow project of schooling as it was played out daily in the classroom, and consider the ways in which this was both paralleled and opposed by children's own views of schooling as a life project.

School is for the future: children's views

Although during fieldwork we did not directly ask the children to consider the purposes of schooling it *was* a question which many of them had already privately considered: why did they have to come to school, what was the point of them having to spend their time there? While some children had reached a fairly cogent answer to these questions, others were still struggling to arrive at a coherent view. This is already suggestive that, for some children, there is a mismatch between the stated purposes of schooling, articulated for them by their teachers, and their personal experience of schooling in terms of the qualitative experience of time spent there. Some children were clear about what school was for. As Marie said, children have to spend time at school so that they can 'get a good education for when you get your job'. Year 6 children saw attending primary school as the first stage in a working life, so it was important to spend time wisely and work hard at primary school, 'so when you go to your secondary school you'll know it all and you can get a good job'. In this sense the main purpose of schooling was in terms of an overall instrumental life plan; school work was regarded as a necessary preparation for the adult world work (see also Sherman 1996). In the following excerpt Sally is reflecting on her experience of school and on the prospect of going to secondary school later in the year. She is very clear about the purpose which school has, linking it firmly to the idea of getting a good job as an adult. She says:

> I want lots of homework . . . cus, you know my big brother, well, he hasn't made much of his life, he's like . . . sits in . . . I don't think he's got a job. . . . I wanna be an actress!

Sally says that if she works hard at school, in effect spending her time wisely, then this will enable her to achieve her ambition to be an actress. She will not be unemployed like her brother who just sits around the house all day. This perspective was also revealed in another conversation with four children:

Pia:	If you could choose, would you then choose to go to school or to work? I mean would you rather be working?
John:	I'd rather go to school.
Bill:	I'd rather go to school.
Elaine:	I'd rather have a job.
John:	Why?
Elaine:	I just would.
Bill:	Well, if you go to school first then you get a better job.
Kelly:	Yeh.
Bill:	And you get more cash, which which do you mean, do you mean primary or college or ?
Pia:	I mean in general, what if you thought, I mean beforehand in England there would be children who would not go to school and they go to work.

Bill: I want to be, when I'm older I want to be a marinologist or marine biologist, work with fish or something and you've got to go to university to do that so.

In these examples the children reveal an awareness of the strategic importance of school in mapping out their life trajectories. In the same vein, as we shall show below, although many of the children complained about having to spend too much time on English and Maths, they also saw these subjects as crucial for their personal futures. As Nigel said, 'Every job you have to do (in adult life), you have to learn to do your maths.'

The achievement of such a utilitarian objective through subjects such as Maths and English, core curriculum subjects, was directly contrasted with lessons such as art and technology. In Tracy's view, 'You don't learn 'owt in art or technology.' These subjects were perceived as less useful by the children, but as we shall see later, for other reasons they were thought enjoyable and valuable. Thus, while many children do acknowledge the necessary temporal investment which they must make in the present, with respect to their future adult life, their daily experience of schooling is sometimes at odds with this sentiment. Charlie, for example, expressed the view that you need to 'get a good education for when you get your job' but when asked whether the process of schooling gives him this experience, his answer was a firm 'No'. In Charlie's experience the view of schooling as a broad, educative life project becomes modified by the everyday and mundane practices of learning. This view, widely shared among children, needs explanation. In order to understand what schooling means to children, therefore, we have to ask not just what children learn at school but how time structures that learning process. The next section explores the structuring of school space by school time.

The social organisation of control over space and time

The three primary schools were in very varied geographical locations, and the arrangement of the constituent parts of the school and the physical condition of the schools also varied, but, although here we consider the spatial organisation of only one of these schools in relation to the structuring of children's time, all three schools worked with comparable demarcations and boundaries to the ones we shall describe.

The school we consider here is in the inner city, built in the 1980s, and comprises three separate buildings. One building constitutes the administrative section and is where the school secretary, the sick bay, the headmaster's study and the staff room are located. The pre-school playgroup also meets here and, in the evening, adult education classes assemble. A second building, designed around a central hexagonal assembly hall, houses the classrooms, while the third building contains the dining hall, the gymnasium and the library. Child-adult relations and the ways in which these are temporally accomplished are inscribed in the conventional and patterned use of these buildings. The administrative building is largely designated as adult space which children only enter at particular times: when they are sick, when they are seeking advice or when they are in trouble. Children who entered this building at other times often became curiously shy as, for example, when, towards the end of play-time, a teacher on duty in the playground would send two pupils to the staff room to warn the teachers that lesson time was about to begin again. Usually, though not always, a pair of girls was chosen for this task. They would, very shyly, enter the short corridor leading to the staff room and stand awkwardly by the open door until they were noticed by a teacher. In their body language they expressed very visibly their fear of possibly being seen to be in the wrong place at the wrong time.

The third building in the city primary school is controlled in its usage by teachers. Children are invited here only at particular times during the school day to carry out particular kinds of activities: having a gym lesson, using the library or eating their dinner. It is only the second building to which children have relatively free access and it is here that children and teachers meet most readily: in lesson time, at the start and end of the school day and as they move between the playground and the classroom.

These different sites in the school are therefore invested with particular kinds of temporal orders through which child–adult relations take place and children's perceptions and understanding of what schools are for is shaped by their knowledge about this time/space relationship. As the children traverse the different spaces of the school building and its environs they acquire or lose certain personal freedoms and control over time use. In this way, they come to understand the child–adult power relations involved in the schooling process as a temporally structured learning experience.

One illustration of this is the ways teachers used time penalties in relation to space, such as the practice of withdrawing the 'privilege' of play-time, which is particularly precious for children. Teachers calculated such punishment minutely; one, two or five minutes would be taken off a child's play-time or, if the teacher thought the misdemeanour severe enough, a child would lose a whole play-time. Martin relates one such occasion when he tried to apologise to his teacher about his part in an argument with another boy in order to escape punishment:

> 'I told her (the teacher) but she made me stay in for five minutes and then she came up to me and goes, "Why did you, why did you say that?" And I said, "I was only telling the truth".'

Taking away children's free time was an effective punishment. Children were made to stay in and continue to work instead of being permitted to play out-side. Indeed, when we asked Steve about the use of time as punishment, he was against suspension from school. This he regarded as a reward, rather than a punishment, for it would give a child lots of free time to spend at home. A better punishment would be instead to impinge on the child's time through converting free time into work time:

'Do you know, instead of getting suspended I'd give them a big folder of homework and what, I want this done by tomorrow then be here at half past ten.'

This, of course, is precisely what teachers do when they punish children by restricting their control over free time at school.

These examples show how the spatial-temporal ordering of the school, and the teachers' paramount control over its social organisation, shape children's everyday experiences. In the next sections we add to this point by exploring the importance for children of having a say over time-use at school and what this indicates about their understandings of the project of schooling.

What is schooling like for children?

That adults and children may have rather different perceptions of school time was apparent in the 'My Week' charts which the children completed for us (Christensen and James 2000). These charts were blank circles which allowed children to represent graphically how they spent their time during a week. Significantly, in their depictions 'school time' was represented as a blank, un-differentiated space. By comparison time spent out of school was usually shown as a variety of different activities (see Figure 6.1).

This bold contrast between school time and home time is highly suggestive of qualitatively different temporal experiences and is, we shall argue, linked to the question of the degree of power and control over time-use which children have in these two spaces. This was illustrated in Pauline's chart (see Figure 6.2).

She was the only one to subdivide 'school time'. She marked out particular shifts in time during the school day: the time travelling between home and school, play-time, lunch-time and time for sports at school; in this way she depicts those time-periods at school over which children, rather than adults, could be said to have a greater degree of control (Blatchford 1998). Thus her chart graphically reflects children's and adults' differential access to time as a resource. Children saw themselves as having little or no control over how to spend time at school: who to sit by, what to wear, who to talk to, when to talk, who to work with and what work to do (see also Pollard et al. 1994). While filling in a decision-making chart, one girl rather pointedly said, 'There's no point [in putting her self on the chart] because they never let you do anything that you say anyway.' This was echoed by Paul:

'You are made to make, do, decisions, it's like 'cos, when you're at home, you can lie back, you can do anything. But when you're at school it's, "You've got to do Maths, you've got to do English, you've got to do that, you've got to do this". I don't really like doing that, I think it's a bit boring but I have to.'

In their understanding of time at school and their relationships with teachers, the children thus confirm Orellana and Thorne's observation that 'those with greater power exert more control over their own time and the time of others' (1998: 17).

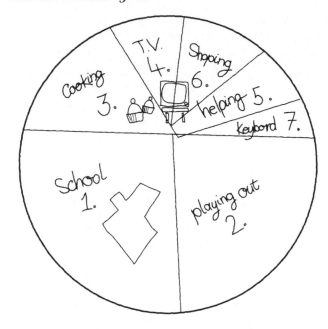

Figure 6.1 'My Week' chart

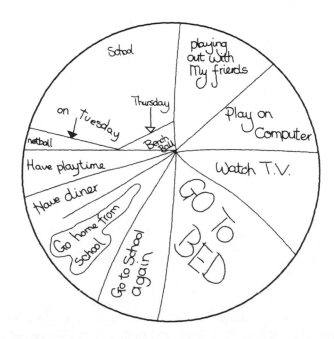

Figure 6.2 'My Week' chart for Pauline

This view of school work and of themselves as powerless in the face of demands upon their time interestingly parallels teachers' own experiences of having to comply with the highly regulated and invasive temporal structures associated with the National Curriculum. In their everyday lives teachers, like children, have to pace their time carefully. Thus Melanie, a teacher at the village school, felt constant pressure on her time. Like all teachers, she had no allocated time for preparation of lessons or for marking children's work, which itself constitutes a heavy workload. Therefore she tended to do all her marking during the break-times and lunch-hour at school. Melanie explains:

'I like to do most of the work at school so I can keep the two things separate. I mean home, family and school. I have my two boys, erm, to concentrate on.'

Melanie was a single mother and used all the time she possibly could at school to do her work. She recognised that working at home needed careful planning and negotiation of time and space with other family members. Children's experience of time at school, as we shall show, mirrors that of their teachers. Teachers encouraged, indeed insisted, that children should 'work hard'; this was starkly illustrated during the week of the SATS tests. Although the children were already recognised by teachers as under a lot of pressure, at one of the village schools, when the children had finished their tests before time, they were told to go back to their classroom, to sit quietly and to start a fresh piece of work.

This expectation of hard work and apparent docile conformity (see Christensen, James and Jenks 2000) has certain costs in terms of what children think schools are for and their experience of the process of schooling. Whilst we do not wish to over-interpret children's pictorial representations of everyday school time, the 'blank space' through which they so often represented it gives pause for thought. It may suggest, for example, that experience of school time was not invested by children with the same value as they gave to schooling as an educational and life project.

In their verbal accounts children confirmed this somewhat negative perception of time at school. When asked about their school day, a common initial response was that school was boring and that therefore the school day often felt very long. Thinking about the days in the week, one boy said, 'School, that's the longest', while another said, 'It seems forever when you're in school.' Maxine was quite clear what the effect this long school day had on her experience of schooling. In a loud and angry voice she said:

'BAD BAD BAD BAD BAD BAD BAD BAD BAD BAD! I wish they'd never had invented it!'

Although few children voiced quite such extreme opinions, spending time at school was not necessarily something they looked forward to, in part because they experienced school as boring. This is clear in the following conversation:

Linda: My mam said that erm you'll want to go to school when you're older though because you like get bored (at work).
Allison: Do you believe her?
Linda: No.
Allison: Why don't you believe her?
Sue: Cos it's boring (at school).

The weekend and days off, in contrast, passed quickly for children precisely because they were *not working,* but most importantly because they could choose what to do. This choice and having a say over time-use is graphically depicted in the 'My Week' chart, where children represented time outside school through a whole range of activities. However, the children's expressed opinion that school is boring has to be tempered for, when pressed to reflect further on their experience of the school day, children made a number of pertinent observations about the ways in which the tempo of the day, and the quality of time passing, changed in relation, for example, to different kinds of work:

> 'When we're doing Maths, it's like three hours. We've got Maths this morning . . . that'll go forever, that.'

However,

> 'When it's like Art, 'n that lot, passes real quick slow . . . once it gets in the afternoon it starts going faster (when you're doing) the good stuff.'

> 'If we've got real good lessons it goes real quick and when we've got really boring lessons it goes (slow).'

> 'When you're enjoying yourself it goes by real fast . . . cos you're enjoying yourself and you don't realise what time it is and it goes too fast really.'

So it is not 'work' per se that children object to, but the type of work and ways of working, over which they see themselves as having little control or choice (see Pollard et al. 1994). The centrality of this became evident in children's expectations about the transition to secondary school. The Year 6 children looked forward to secondary school precisely because they thought there would be more activities and facilities and therefore that they would have more choice and say over how they spent their time. Boredom at school is, thus, we would argue, a reflection of children's weak position vis-à-vis teachers in the decisions they can make about time-use; after all, one would not voluntarily choose to spend one's time doing boring things!

Time-shifting

Although children's everyday control over time at school is limited, they nonetheless have strategies for time-control which mean they do not perceive themselves to be ultimately subordinated by the temporal ordering of the school day (see Chapter 3 for discussion of coping strategies). Children were, for example, well aware of teachers casting their gaze over the activities taking place in the playground – keeping their eyes open for children who might try sneakily to stay inside the classroom during play-time. Children had to be out-side in the playground and were only allowed to stay inside when it was rain-ing ('wet play-times') or to finish their schoolwork. However, although children acknowledged teachers' overarching control over time at school, break-times gave children scope to control how they spent their time. Tim, one of the boys in Year 6 at the inner city school explained:

> 'Play-time . . . there's usually a teacher on play-times, so you (if you) get into trouble, so, they decide what you do at play-time. *They don't decide if you're gonna play football, or if you don't behave*' (our emphasis).

The importance of having some control over one's time can be further illus-trated by children's accounts of their strategies to control time. This we call 'time-shifting'. For example, although time at school is often experienced by children as passing slowly, they were aware that the tempo of the day, that is their *experience* of time passing, was something which, in part, could be con-trolled by them. It could be changed through their own attitudes towards the work they were doing. Two boys, who were both slow readers with poor literacy skills were perceptive about this relationship. Bob said, '(English goes slowly) because you have to work your mind too much, strain your mind . . . and you have to write real quick and do spellings and stuff in our special group'. And the other boy, Clive, describes how he could alter the tempo of the day by changing his own behaviour: '(Time goes) slowly, when you don't like the work, what you're doing and you write real quickly and the time flies by more or less'.

Time can also be stretched out or given over to other activities, thus reduc-ing teachers' apparent control over how children spend their time at school:

Chris: They can't like *make* me do work.
Allison: So that's when you think you've got some control . . . cos you can actually choose whether you do it . . . and if you choose not to do it and you get into trouble, that's your choice. Is that what you mean?
Chris: Yeah. You can do, in some work you can decide what I want to do. (sic)

Thus, although, as we suggest, time at school would seem to be largely regu-lated by teachers and by the formalities of the time-table, children do see themselves as exercising some control over that temporal regulation. This works at the most micro of levels, for, as Ian described to us, the position and placement of the desk in the classroom can alter the way in which time is experienced. Sitting facing the classroom wall on which the clock was hung, he said:

> 'I hate looking this way 'cos you're like looking this way and your eyes are always pointing to the clock and then your belly starts grumbling. Like at twelve or quarter to twelve, got to eat'.

Other children adopted a similar strategy of ignoring time during 'boring lessons'. They, too, purposefully did not look at the clock, because, as Susie said, 'you don't know what time it is and the time flies'. Close observation of the pre-assembly period in the city school revealed similar time-shifting strategies at work. This 30 minute period at the beginning of the day was a valued 'breathing' space for children. It was relatively unstructured and unsupervised, not quite a lesson and yet not play-time, a time when children were supposed to sit and read quietly while the teacher was busy doing the register. However, what children actually did in this time varied considerably. Some children did read; others got out their reading books, opened them and then sat lost in thought or whispered to their friends; others huddled around the book shelves, ostensibly to choose a new book, but never taking one down; others fiddled with their pencil cases, or with their hair, had their books open in front of them but never turned a page; still others wandered around the room, looking busy, as they ferreted in their trays or searched the resources table. A small number of children, however, sat at their tables with no books visible, or talked openly with their friends. Thus, out of the class of thirty-five children maybe only ten might be 'sitting and reading' for the whole period of time. Such time-shifting strategies gives children the experience of having a say over the way in which time at school is spent and structured and was an occasional secret pleasure shared and celebrated by children.

Conclusion

We have shown the practical ways in which the project of schooling for teachers and children both comes together and diverges in terms of their expectations of what schools are for. These differences, which may lead to conflicts about schooling, are shaped through the everyday interactions between adults and children at school. Central to this, we have argued, is the temporal and spatial ordering of the school over which adults claim the greatest power and control. This explains why, although children are concerned to get a good education and to engage with school work, they nonetheless experience the schooling process as 'boring'. The disincentives are the lack of control which children feel themselves to have over how and with whom they spend their time. In this the question of choice and having a say is crucial and within the confines of the primary classroom children exercise their control over time through time-shifting practices. An indication of the importance children place on decisions over time-use in their relationships with adults can be seen in the positive, but possibly naive expectation which all the children had about secondary school. There, they thought, they would have more say over how they spent their time and thus their experiences at school would have a more meaningful place in their everyday lives.

Notes

1 This project was carried out, together with Chris Jenks, on the Economic and Social Research Council Children 5–16 Programme, under the title: 'Changing Times: Children's understanding and perception of the social organisation of time.'

2 This question is also central to Ann Sherman's (1996) enquiry into 5 year old children's views on their first year at primary school.

3 This contrasts with Sherman's (1996) study of children in their first year at primary school, which showed that even when the children were unhappy with some aspects of their schooling, they did not question the value which school has. They believed that 'whatever school situation they were in was appropriate for them and, therefore a good school' (1996: 40).

4 SATS stands for Standard Assessment Tests. These are national tests, administered at age 7 and 10–11 in primary schools, and used to assess how well both children and the schools are doing.

5 OFSTED stands for Office for Standards in Education. This privatised inspection service has been established to monitor school performance and suggest remedies where appropriate.

7 Culture and childhood in pastoralist communities: the example of Outer Mongolia

Helen Penn

Introduction – theoretical context for the enquiry

Within my own discipline of child development, parents, carers and key adults in children's lives are seen as the main agents of socialization and mediators of culture, and as such, their attitudes and behaviour have been examined in order to assess their impact on their children. Many of the more recent volumes are cross-cultural and refer to the range of variation of styles of parenting, and these styles are explained partly as a matter of cultural adaptation to the required norms of the society (Belle 1989; Goodnow and Collins 1990; Bornstein 1991; Harkness and Super 1996). Mostly these studies are undertaken from the stance that parents shape and critically determine their children's lives, particularly in early childhood, rather than exploring how children may be active agents and arbiters of their own lives. This kind of psychological analysis also focuses on individual performance; that is these studies do not view children as a social group subject to certain political and social pressures by virtue of their childhood.

Child development offers a particular, micro-level approach to interpreting the activities of children, which has been criticized both for its narrowness and for the universality implicit in its definitions of childhood (Burman 1994). Yet whichever discipline you take – psychology, sociology, history, biology or medicine – or even anthropology – most of the research and most of the thinking about children and childhood has been done in or from a particular Euro-American context. The issue is not only which kind of discipline might reveal insights about childhood and being a child, but also *where* that discipline originates and is pursued.

America constitutes about 5 per cent of the world's population, Western Europe a further 12 per cent – in other words they cover a *minority* of the world's children. The *majority* of the world's children live in South America, Asia and Africa, and many if not most of this majority live in very different circumstances from the minority. They live in situations of rural isolation or urban degradation, in highly collective settings, with few material goods, where the recognition of and satisfaction of individual needs, wants and choices is mostly inconceivable. For many children, the services which in the minority world we take for granted and think of as a right, in education and healthcare, sanitation and transport, fuel and power supply and food security, either do not exist or are too costly to purchase. Self-reliance and subsistence are the only options for their families or communities. I hesitate to use conventional words like poverty or deprivation to describe such circumstances, because they imply a linear model of development and progress, one which is increasingly questioned (Sachs 1992). Instead we need to question pervasive minority world assumptions about childhood and child development, children's rights, learning and education, which originate from and represent a particular and very powerful world view; but can only with distortion be generalized to the majority of children in the world.

How then does one define culture, over and above the distinction between majority and minority world? Culture is often viewed as a bounded and essentially changeless and seamless web of customs, rituals and practices which characterize a particular group of people in a particular geographical location. This conservative view of culture has been challenged, most notably by Rosaldo (1993). He argues that the 'culture' of any group always contains inherent contradictions and uncertainties and is always discursive and struggling; and these contradictions and uncertainties are amplified when people perceive themselves as subordinate to other groups who are more powerful – such as Europeans and Americans. Rosaldo claims most of the world's people inhabit 'cultural borderlands', that is, they are acutely aware of the contradictions they face in moving between dominant (minority) and subordinate (majority) perspectives. This more radical model of culture has also been vividly expressed by the Kenyan novelist Ngugi wa Thiongi'o (1993):

> Culture develops within the process of a people wrestling with their natural and social environment. They struggle with nature. They struggle with one another. They evolve a way of life embodied in their institutions and certain practices. Culture becomes the carrier of their moral, aesthetic and ethical values. At the psychological level, these values become the embodiment of the people's consciousness as a specific community . . . Within a given community any change in the major aspect of their lives, how they manage their wealth for instance, or their power, may well bring about changes at all the other levels and these in turn will bring about mutual action and reaction on all the other aspects. Here there is no stillness but constant movement and the problem about study of cultures . . . is how to study them in their movement and linkages to other processes in that society or community. It is like studying a river in its very movement . . . (p. 29)

Kagitcibasi (1996) is one of the few psychologists who wrestles with the idea of context and culture from a majority world perspective. Her argument is that we can be clearer in distinguishing between biological and environmental influences on children if we make systematic cross-cultural comparisons. In her own work she argues that a crucial dimension along which societies and cultures vary is that of dependence-independence. The notion of the bounded individual self is a peculiarly western one.

> The more individualistic the culture (i.e. the more the self is construed as separate) the more frequent is the sampling of the private self (i.e. the self is more salient in a person's experience) and conversely, the more collectivist the culture, the more collective self is sampled. (p. 63)

Whilst sympathetic to its insights, she does not accept the relativist view that context is infinitely complex and all encompassing. In particular, she argues that in a global economy the pressures on the most marginal peoples are such that they have to adapt to external, international standards, for example the requirement to become literate; but that the most effective way of supporting and teaching children from such marginal backgrounds is to do so in a way which acknowledges and works within their particular cultural context. Where the context is a collectivist one, then approaches which preserve and emphasize social relations are likely to be the most successful, at least in terms of individual learning.

The childhood I describe in this chapter is that of Mongolian pastoralist communities in the Gobi Desert. Pastoralist and nomadic communities are often regarded as amongst the most geographically, economically and politically peripheral in the world, although in fact their integration with broader socio-political and economic forces is consistently underestimated, and they have always had to adapt to survive and prosper (Chang and Koster 1994). Mongolia is a particularly interesting case of a pastoralist society. It is one of the world's poorest countries, and has an exceptionally harsh climate, but as an ex-client state of the Soviet Union, it experienced a massive drive for education and health, and the imposition of a communist ideology over the seventy years of 1921–90. By 1990, over 90 per cent of the population was schooled and literate, although the overwhelming majority either are still pastoralists, or are within a generation of being so. The experiences of the children I met provide a useful example of the tensions described above, between collectivist-individual, dependent/interdependent understandings of daily life, and between the pressures of a traditional pastoralist life, and the external demands of a global economy (see Chapter 3 for discussion of children's participation in a different subsistence household economy).

Sources of information

My information is drawn from a number of sources. I have been visiting Mongolia since 1996 on behalf of Save the Children UK, to act as an external adviser to the Ministry of Education and Culture on the sustainability of its kindergarten system. As a result I have had access to schools and kindergartens, where I have observed and spoken to groups of children, as well as holding conversations with teachers and officials. I have visited and observed in ger[1] households and kept a photographic record of my visits. I also have a number of key informants: Demberel, who was previously a herder in the Gobi but is now Director of Education for Gobi Altai region;[2] and Mandal and Tsendserin, who work for Save the Children in the capital city, Ulaan Baator. I have had many discussions with them about childhood and children's needs, which have continued over e-mail, and Mandal and Tsendserin have also visited me for periods in London, where we have resumed our discussions and comparisons. Demberel, at my request, has also written a brief (unpublished) autobiography, in which he describes his own childhood, and his aspirations for the children for whom he is now responsible. I have also been able to use education, health and demographic statistics (Mongolian National University 1994; National Statistical Board, Mongolia 1996; Ministry of Enlightenment, Mongolia 1996; Government of Mongolia 1993). There is also a substantial literature on Mongolia, some of it ancient (Cleaves 1982); some of it scholarly accounts of travels in the 1920s (Lattimore 1941); and much of it contemporary in the form of reports from development agencies such as the World Bank (1996), the Government of Mongolia, with the help of UNICEF (1993) and the Asian Development Bank (1995).

What I am presenting therefore is a composite account of childhood, which includes adult reminiscences and commentaries, as well as observations of children and children's own views, and which is grounded in a socio-demographic analysis of the current situation of Mongolia.

Mongolian society

Mongolia is traditionally a nomadic, pastoralist society. Families own herds of animals – sheep, goats, cows, horses and camels – and move around with them, on prescribed routes and in prescribed arcs, to find suitable grazing. In the Gobi, where the temperature ranges from −40C in winter, to +40C in summer, winter habitations are semi-permanent, whereas in spring and early summer herders may need to move every three to ten days to find suitable grazing and water. A viable number of animals cannot fall much below ten cows and thirty sheep plus horses and/or camels for transport; but richer herders will have up to 2000 animals.

Mongolia was a communist country, and under the communist regime, a kind of collective system was evolved. From the 1930s, the herders were organized into Negdels or collectives; they continued to be pastoralists and to move in search of grazing, but the number and type of animals they herded were negotiated within the Negdel. Moreover the Negdel organized *sum* or district level centres, where a number of services were provided – basic medicine and veterinary services, boarding school education for children of 8–16, outreach adult education, emergency fodder supplies for harsh winters, sales outlets for animal produce, and so on (Goldstein and Beall 1994). Since the fall of communism, the Negdels have been disbanded, and the herders are on their own. If they want any of the services they previously took for granted, they must now pay for them, including education. The result has been that the herders have retreated into the desert, and built up their herds as the only security they have. There has been a dramatic increase in the number of animals. The animals need looking after, and the only resource for doing so is the children. So children who previously might have expected to go to school, are now kept at home to herd the extra animals. The drop out rate from school has been considerable, for boys rather than girls. Many of the boarding schools now have 10–20 girls for every boy. Mongolia achieved a 96 per cent literacy rate under communism, and literacy is still valued – but there are other more pressing needs for survival.

What is herding life like for children? This is Demberel's description:

> My father Lodi is a typical herdsman and my family is one of many (fifty or so) families that live year round in the crest, valleys and pasture land of the Khar Azarga range in the Altai mountains. My father gained experience handed down from generation to generation . . . he was literate and had much practice in husbandry and felt-making. He could cure sick animals, and apply first aid to a person poisoned by a poisonous plant . . . My mother Khumban can read, do arithmetic problems in her head, and has raised 6 children. My mother makes dairy products, curd, skimmed milk and dried products, and sews clothing and makes footwear . . . Till the age of eight I was living with my parents, herding flocks of sheep and goats, helping them with the daily work, playing with my contemporaries and enjoying the beauty of the land.

Many children grow up in extreme isolation 50 km or more across the desert or steppe to even the smallest *sum* (settlement) where there is a primary school. Families live in gers. A ger, or small cluster of gers, typically houses an extended family – mother, father, grandparents, unmarried aunts or uncles, children until they are married, nephews, nieces and cousins. Single parents, men or women, cannot survive on their own in the desert; there is too much work to do, so they will usually move in with other relatives. Children in order to go to school in the *sum* centre may stay with relatives in the *sum*, or else become school boarders. Or conversely, children from larger towns or from Ulaan Baator, the capital city of Mongolia, might be sent to live with relatives in the ger. The household therefore, as well as being nomadic, also has a fluctuating population. Sometimes children who are not kin also seem to reside in the ger. For example in one ger I visited, a small child of about 6 years crouched silently near the door, ran to fetch water for the kettle, and carried out small tasks. 'Is he your youngest?' I enquired of the woman in the ger. 'No, he is from another ger, he just comes to visit.' As there was no other ger within eyesight across the desert, I wondered about the nature of the visit, the independence of action it might imply. (However, closer questioning would have been perceived as rude.)

Since the climate is so harsh, the ger is much more than a night shelter. It is a daily living space for the family, and is well equipped with iron or wooden bedsteads, a collapsible metal stove, cupboards, shelves, and a variety of cooking implements including very large pots and pans for making and refining milk products. It may also have radios and displays of family photos – and even a television when they are in a winter quarters. With so many people and so many things in a small space, many daily activities are governed by ritual – possessions are always placed in the ger in the same configurations, and people enter and exit in prescribed ways.

Children's daily life

Within this heavily prescribed setting there is very little possibility and very few openings for children to be boisterous or to intrude on adult occupations or conversations. Very young children are nursed almost continuously on an adult's lap, older children are at all times encouraged and shown how to be supportive and kind to younger children. The kind of sibling rivalry which we take for granted is firmly and systematically discouraged, as is any display of self-will. Instead the supportive, helpful role of children is continually emphasized by word and gesture. Inside the ger, children sit cross-legged on the floor and are expected to watch and listen to adult conversation – and they must also learn what not to see and hear. Intimacy is indicated by turning away and speaking very quietly, and when adults speak and act like this, children must switch off their attention.

Children are taught to be respectful of the adults around them, and not to venture their own opinions or feelings. Mandal sent me a code of practice recently drawn up by researchers in Ulaan Baator which attempted to record and codify the traditional relationships between adults and children which had been, in the researchers' view, obscured by communism and which needed to be restated as a foundation for post-communist Mongolia. Urunge Onon, a Mongolian writer reminiscing about his childhood in the 1920s, wrote that:

> Parents drilled into their children a deep-seated respect for their elders; they had to respect all members of an older generation . . . very elderly people however were treated by the utmost respect and courtesy by all. Wealth or poverty or position in life had nothing to do with this. According to the thinking of our people, honours and riches were bestowed by mere men, but ripe old age is a gift from heaven. For this reason no-one made any attempt to conceal his or her advancing years. On the contrary, all could look forward to that golden autumnal period of life, when full of years and rich experience of living, they would receive that special respect and consideration which would be their greatest reward. (1972: 9)

As with some other nomadic groups living in harsh circumstances, physical survival depends on achieving harmony; on being incurious about the actions and motives of others – hence the difficulties in asking questions (Briggs

1970). This contrasts very much with what we know about Anglo–American child-rearing. For example Judy Dunn (1996), who is noted for her research into the socialization of children within the family, comments that: '. . . children in England and the US grow up in a world in which the actions' feelings, intentions, wants, beliefs and knowledge of people are continually discussed' (p. 86).

These kinds of discussions about intentionality, it is claimed, lead to children developing theories of mind, to their accurate perceptions of others. But, as various writers on nomadism have pointed out, rather than place oneself in relation to others, the emphasis is on placing oneself in a terrain (Monbiot 1994). The shamanistic religions of north east Asia, now slowly reviving after their suppression during communism, reflect this integration of the person with the landscape (Humphrey 1996). One of the most acute observers of Mongolian life, Owen Lattimore (1941) describes the perceptual skills necessary to place oneself in a landscape.

> . . . we always look for standard shapes and sizes, while they are skilled in watching for movement, changing colour, a new angle of light. When you cannot say for sure whether the distance is a few hundred yards or a mile it may be hard to know whether you are looking at a white boulder not very far away or a round white felt tent much further away. It is not exactly accuracy of sight that tells you the difference: instead of straining for the detail of the white object alone you must look at what goes with it, at the whole setting. If it is a tent and if there is a cross light you might be able to see converging on the tent the trails by which the cattle come home; you might be able to see the movement of people or dogs, though you could not say whether it was a man or a dog that moved. Even if the light does not favour you it is often possible to estimate by the configuration of the land as a whole whether it is a place where you might find a tent or a place where people would not be likely to camp. (p. 209)

Children are expected to share in the herding tasks as soon as they can, and these tasks are gender differentiated, as Demberel's account illustrates. Girls typically help with the activities around the ger, preparing food and animal products, and collecting dung for fuel. Boys help with the herding. In one of the group sessions in the school, several of the younger boys (aged 6 or 7 years) told us that their job was 'to follow the sheep'. I said I did not know how to do such a job, and could one of them explain to me how it was done? Did they have to show the sheep where to go? Find them water? Protect them against wolves and other predators? The children found it very difficult to explain what they did. But it gradually emerged that, except during the worst winter months, generally a child herder will be out at dawn with the flock, and return with them at dusk, the child being without any food or drink or provisions whilst he is away from the ger. I wondered if I had misunderstood the children, so harsh did the life seem, but Demberel confirmed that this was how he and many of his friends were brought up. One special job in the spring is to collect up new born or vulnerable animals in an especially designed sack and bring them back to the rough corral next to the ger where they could be watched. We came across several young boys walking across the desert steppes holding such sacks.

Both boys and girls were utterly familiar with young animals. We watched young children playing with calves, kids and baby camel in the corral, holding them, wriggling alongside them, teasing them. Lattimore (1941) points out how the nature of this inter-relationship between animals and humans is determined by nomadism.

> Every family has its own camping grounds and allotted range of pasture within the territory but there is no individual property in land and nothing except human control to keep herds from wandering all over creation. The human control and association must therefore be moderate, patient and unremitting . . . to be a good nomad you must accommodate yourself to your animals as much as you subordinate them to you. (p. 170)

Horses and camels are the main form of transport, although a few wealthier families have motorized bikes or trucks. The horses are semi-wild and extremely tough. They are brown, grey or white, or any combination of these colours. (In fact there are 320 different colour names for horses, and by school age a child would be expected to know most, if not all of them – a subtlety of recognition which contrasts with our own crude notion of primary colours.) Children will learn to handle and ride horses and camels very early on. Demberel remembered his first trip to school in the *sum:*

> We headed off 20 kms away to the 'bag' the smallest administrative unit (of the settlement area) accompanied by father. As everyone rides a horse, we would race. Commonly, a Mongolian child at the age of 5 rides fast horses.

Children from pastoralist communities in the Gobi, then, live in shifting kinship groups, where they are expected to be unquestioningly respectful of others. They are expected to share in the herding work of the household, and the work is assigned to them on the basis of gender. They know animals intimately. Their work responsibilities are very arduous. They have learnt to be physically very tough, and to withstand hunger and thirst, and extreme heat and cold. They can assess and weigh the balance of all kinds of variations in their environment.

Schooling

What happens when – and if – these children reach school? Under communism, all children were expected to be schooled and it was exceptional for a child to miss school. Many, like Demberel, went on to tertiary education. Each *sum* settlement runs a village school for children 8–14, and usually there is also a kindergarten for the children of the *sum* workers. Children either board at the school, or else stay with relatives in the *sum*. Demberel remembers his schooldays vividly.

> The beginning period of studying was unusual for me, as someone generally used to living in a solitary ger in pasture land. It was especially unusual to be among contemporaries in a room with smells and colours and to study lessons. It has left precious, unforgettable recollections in my memory. I studied there for four years. For the first two years my sister and myself lived with my uncle and the following two years in the school dormitory.
>
> My first school was in a little settlement in semi-desert. There were about ten people working in it: a teacher, doctor, guard, stoker and some other workers. It consisted of two little white houses: a school and a dormitory. As I was living with relatives, in my free time I used to carry water, herd the flock, collect fuel, dung, and prepare food. I think the days passed quickly. In the dormitory children would play and study, so the days seemed longer and boring. Occasionally at the weekends, or for holidays, we would go home. Homesickness was one of our big problems. A few among us would be discouraged and run away. But the one thing that made us survive was our knowledge that the teacher, cook, guard, president (of the commune) were all doing everything possible for us. In the dormitory they provided us completely with bed clothes, sanitary-wares, made our food and even the stoker and cook bathed us and washed our dirty clothes. Gradually through those people's love we became accustomed to the school. It is not an easy thing to be away during one's childhood, from home. Every countryside child overcomes this.

School is an awesome place for the youngest children. Children may wear their very best – or only – respectable clothes for school, and indeed parents said to us many times that one of the things they valued about school was that it was a place where children could keep clean – unlike home where they could not. Many children are very shy and tongue-tied when they first come to school, and find it very difficult to talk to adults. The communist education system itself depressed enquiry and criticism. It was almost entirely didactic, relying on the transmission of prescribed knowledge through a centralized curriculum. The very body language of children and their parents indicates submission.

However, this school system is changing. The end of the communist era in 1990 has led to the wholesale adoption of market economics (Asian Development Bank 1995; World Bank 1996), and all families must now pay for food and lodging in order for their children to attend school. In addition, as many communal responsibilities and jobs disappear, those families who can have built up their herds as a security in the new economic climate. In some of the gers we visited, the parents might be relatively well qualified – for example one woman herder we met had a veterinary degree – but needed to keep their children at home to help with the herding. The helpful loving attitudes of school staff remembered by Demberel are less and less common, and he is concerned about the transition process.

> The people deeply respected Mongolian traditions and nationality and had a high sense of duty. These two factors were the main reasons why the education programme was successful. Now people criticize this state centralism. I consider it still as a humanitarian policy done for the wellbeing of the country, right for the people when we were so backward . . . Teachers would be on duty at all hours, they would be there at mealtimes, wake children up, put them to bed. Teachers were responsible for discipline as a whole, which included paying attention to the hygiene of the students . . . They took their duties very seriously . . . the salary of the teachers was high compared to other people's so they paid attention to the work.

Now teachers' salaries are very low, and the pioneering enthusiasm has gone. But also problems of dependency and, for Demberel, all sorts of previously depressed concerns have emerged.

> Mongolians who live in a vast steppe and live in a nomadic tradition face lots of difficulties in the education process. First of all children in their early ages lived separately from parents, and under the pressure of homesickness they couldn't concentrate on learning and do well. They were away from their parents' love and did not need to undertake daily work, and consequently became used to living a ready-made life. They grew soft and were tempted towards a corrupt life, one which ignored traditional Mongolian approaches to child rearing. They became passive and lost the initiative and the ability to find innovative solutions.

Demberel, as a person of some standing in his community, is influenced by arguments put forward by international development agencies about the future of Mongolia.

> The Democratic Revolution began in 1990 and the mode of life of the country has been completely changed in a short period of time. Since we have realized that democracy, human rights, liberty, the principles of a free economy are the ultimate goals of humanity, we abolished the former political and economic system of social and intellectual life and now we are under way in realizing a new political system, establishing the basis of democracy and the transition to a market economy.

The Government has determined the aim of education and endorsed a new educational law. According to world trends, a big education renovation process has been started based on the achievements of the past seventy year experiment. Education in our country has been too ideological and the study process was based on the needs of society rather than on the interests or desires of the individual. It was too theorized and removed from practice and usage and its management is very centralized. We are in the process of changing this.

Demberel's concerns about the education system have also been echoed by a research study into schooling carried out by a Danish team (Holst et al. 1996). Madsen, one of the team, interviewed children about their views of schooling. She commented that it was very difficult to persuade children to talk.

> The children were completely unaccustomed to questions asking for their own views about school, society and their own lives . . . this does not mean that children are not loved and respected . . . but it reflects a tradition of upbringing in which the position and role of children are controlled by the adult world – but it is a world of which they are an integral and natural part . . . Unlike the Western middle classes, Mongolian parents do not regard their children as projects. (Holst et al. 1996, p. 78)

But Madsen did persuade some of the older and more articulate children to speak to her. As with some of the adolescents interviewed by Kagitcibasi (1996) who also came from more collectivist societies, the comments Madsen elicited were almost entirely to do with the children's altruistic concerns about the future of their families and their country during and after transition. As well as the adoption of new ideologies, transition has had the immediate effect for most children of a huge drop in their families' living standards, and they are worried about how their families will cope.

> When there is a market economy there is also democracy. I read that in the paper. It is us who are going to decide. But we can't decide very much if we don't know what to decide about. That's why education is so important . . . Lots of pupils have dropped out of school. There was one boy who was very clever but his family decided that he had to tend the animals. That's because some people think that if children don't get good marks they might as well leave school. But they get bad marks because they don't have the textbooks, or because they don't have time to do their homework. So they just have to leave. I think it's very unfair, it's very very bad for the children and for our country. (p. 85)

I have read a lot in the papers about what happened in Mongolia and in my society after the upheavals of 1989. Before there was political oppression in our country – I know that now but I didn't know it before. Now we are free – but the prices are so high that people became poor. That is because we have a market economy . . . We are a little people. If we don't develop our production we will disappear as a people. You can already see this in lots of places. There are many people in the streets who are very drunk. It wasn't like that before and it makes me afraid. (p. 90)

In most majority world countries, schooling requires children to be bilingual, or trilingual, learning a local, regional and international language. Many of the *sum* schools had switched from teaching Russian as a second language to teaching English, which is now the language of development aid. The seriousness with which it is regarded was illustrated for me by a visit to a rather scruffy and overflowing ger an hour's travel from the nearest *sum*. In anticipation of our visit everyone from the cluster of family gers had arrived. Nineteen people including children were packed into the ger! The children of all ages behaved impeccably and sat very still. The herder woman, now a grandmother, had eleven children, most of whom had in turn become herders. But the eleventh child, a girl, was taking an English degree in Ulaan Baator.

I was asked at almost all the *sum* schools if I would talk in English to the children studying English. I tried to use these sessions as an opening for conversation, but the textbooks from which the children had rehearsed their English were somewhat stilted. 'What is your hobby?' I was asked. I ruled out gardening and reading as a conversational response, since neither were possible in the desert steppes, and said I liked watching birds. 'Do you have a hobby?' I asked in turn. 'I collect coins' was the rather surprising answer. Later I had a discussion with Tsendserin about whether 'hobby' was a translatable concept. I thought the textbook inappropriate, but Tsendserin was indignant, and said that there were many beautiful old coins still circulating, and it was a good hobby! It remained an unpursued point as to whether the children we met had sufficient concepts of self and privacy – and time and money – to develop individual tastes and interests like this, but I use it as an example of the kinds of changes of attitude implicitly expected of children at school, apparently trivial, but with enormous implications.

Conclusion

Mongolian pastoralist life is just one example of the many different conditions in which children grow up. It is a lifestyle which is unrecognizable to those of us grounded in minority world notions of choice, privacy, comfort and safety, and it was almost unbearable to me for the very short time I lived it. But in addition to learning to live a pastoralist life, Mongolian children have had to negotiate macro-change; first communism, and now a market rhetoric. Paradoxically, at the same time, many families are retreating into a more traditional and isolated lifestyle, or failing to cope with the changes required of them, so the processes of micro-change, at a family level, are becoming more problematic. The numbers of street children in Ulaan Baator are generally taken as a sign of family breakdown. From having had no street children before transition, there are now hundreds.

Children in Mongolia will have to come to terms with the powerfulness of minority world images and its linguistic imperatives; with the mirages of freedom and choice and the more traditional views of the collectivist society in which they were raised. These contradictions of past and present, obligation and self-fulfilment, work and leisure, frugality and wealth beyond the dreams of avarice, are faced by children all over the world except perhaps in our own minority world enclaves where we paradoxically assume that we alone face profound and rapid change.

Notes

1 A ger is a circular tent constructed of a white felt covering over a flexible wooden lattice frame.
2 A reasonably common example of social mobility under communism.

8   Some Sydney children define abuse: implications for agency in childhood

Jan Mason and Jan Falloon

Introduction – background to the study

The adult-centric discourses on abuse

Child abuse and the development of systems to protect children from abuse, has been a major focus of attention in all western and to an increasing extent non-western countries during the twentieth century. Discourses on child abuse in Australia have followed developments in the United States and also the United Kingdom with the positivist medico-legal model being dominant. This discourse has constructed child abuse as an objective social problem about which something can and should be done. Child protection professionals, as the adult experts on child abuse, have decided who are the abusers and defined them as pathological. They have placed these abusers under surveillance or removed their children, defined as victims.

The discourses around child abuse and solutions to it have both reflected and played a key part in articulating the roles of state and family in relation to the child. In Australia, as in other developed countries, the relationship between state and family as codified in law and institutions has been influenced by the notion of the 'ideal patriarchal family of the industrialised middle class in nineteenth century Britain' (Rayner 1996: 34). In this relationship the functioning of families within normative parameters has generally been free from public scrutiny, with the state only intervening where families have been considered to have failed.

Consensus is lacking on what is child abuse (Gough 1996), even though most child protection interventions and most legislation against child abuse have developed as if there were consensus. Professionals have typically determined what is abusive to children on the basis of the dominant social science paradigm, which has focused on children as becoming adults. Within this paradigm decisions have been made about what is in children's best interests on the basis of what professionals consider will promote development into a normative healthy adulthood. The concern has been for children as the adults of tomorrow because 'ultimately our children's future and our world's future are one' (Kempe and Kempe 1978: 148).

From within this framework, Australian child protection policy has historically emphasised 'normative' familial arrangements and the control of deviancy. Interventions regarding child abuse into families considered to have failed, have typically been focused on poor, lower class, frequently sole parent and Aboriginal, or other marginalised groups (Mason and Noble-Spruell 1993). A corollary has been that families functioning within normative parameters have been generally free from public scrutiny. For a brief time in the 1970s, these families came under the microscope, as a consequence of feminist critique which highlighted the way in which patriarchal relations camouflaged the extent of familial child sexual abuse. An alternative paradigm was asserted for understanding and responding to child sexual abuse. However, in implementing policy to confront child sexual abuse, the basic tenets of the medico-legal approach again dominated and the resultant strategies emphasised the reporting and investigating of individual cases of sexual abuse.

Aspects of the broader Australian social policy context regarding children

The emphasis of Australian child abuse and child protection policies on the most marginalised, has been paralleled by a limited focus by government at both national or state levels, on the social and economic rights of children and young people. In terms of government support to children and their families, Australia has been placed on a continuum of public–private responsibility for children, somewhere between European countries, such as Sweden and France on the one hand and the United States on the other (Funder 1996). Community attitudes in Australia to the rights of children can be similarly located as between extremes. It is significant that the Convention of the Rights of the Child, while ratified by Australia after much public debate, 'has not been incorporated, legislatively, into federal legislation as other human rights instruments have been' (Rayner 1995: 190).

In a recent (1998) government committee inquiry into the United Nations Convention on the Rights of the Child in Australia, submissions were called for from the public. Of the submissions received just over half (51 per cent) did not support the Convention. In submissions supportive of the Convention the focus was on the inadequacy of current administrative legislative mechanisms for addressing the needs of children and Australia's lack of compliance with and breaches of the Convention (McLelland 1998). Physical punishment of children is still legal in Australia.

The current lack of a national organisation responsible for addressing children's needs or focusing on their rights as identified in the Convention, contrasts with the considerable attention currently being paid by Australian politicians and the media to law and order policies targeted at children and young people. Concern with the controlling of children has been made explicit in recent years in legislation to limit the use by children of public spaces. Such policies have considerable public support in a country where the most controversial aspects of the Convention, as expressed in the submissions to the government inquiry, were those relating to 'the autonomous child' and to the 'physical harm/punishment' of children (McLelland 1998: 2).

In this context it is not surprising that children's voices and their know-ledge are typically given little space in the media and in public decision making, even where their interests are directly concerned. While children are the focus of research and policy on child abuse, the broader failure to take children seriously or to acknowledge that they can be either 'knowers or agents of knowledge' (John 1996: 10), extends to child abuse and protection matters (Cashmore, Dolby and Brennan 1995; Mason 1993). In Australia, as in other industrialised countries, children's voices have until very recently been missing from the discourses as conducted in the literature and in public forums.

The adult-centred discourse which has dominated child abuse and protec-tion research and policy, centres on children as 'becoming' adults rather than 'beings'. In this process children's subjectivities are typically ignored and their experiences are of being treated as objects, as silent victims for whom others, professionals, must speak (Mason and Noble-Spruell 1993; Cashmore, Dolby and Brennan 1995). These professionals decide what is child abuse and how to respond to it.

Towards (ac)knowledging children's standpoints on abuse

In Australia in those forums where children's voices and the voices of those who have experienced child protection interventions as children, have been listened to, children have spoken out about the abusiveness of the system designed to protect them from abuse (Mason 1993; Owen 1996; Cashmore, Dolby and Brennan 1995; New South Wales Child Protection Council 1998). There is a lack of formal research reporting on children's perspectives of abuse, where the children are not already a part of the child protection system, or defined as 'at risk'. In the one known study (Butler and Williamson 1994), where views of children *not* in care were sought in addition to the views of children in care, the researchers focused on the definition of 'significant harm', as used in the England and Wales *Children Act 1989*. The views of chil-dren reported in this research challenged adult interpretations of abuse. In particular, they demonstrated clear differences between children's definition of what they define as 'safety' and adult definitions of what they define as 'protection'.

In our study, we sought children's standpoint(s). Feminists, in contributing to knowledge from women's standpoint(s), sought, as the basis for challenging women's 'scientific non-being', to identify and document women's own sub-jective experiences (Mies 1991: 66). When we came to exploring and docu-menting the experiences of children from their standpoints we faced a major obstacle. The very possibility of children having 'experience' tends to be denied. Adult-imposed hierarchies of knowledge equate experience with adulthood. Exploring children's experiences directly challenges the needs and interests of what Dorothy Smith (1999: 77) describes as 'ruling relations'. In the case of children, these 'ruling relations' are adults and their construction of adulthood, as the possession of maturity and reality.

In seeking to obtain children's standpoint(s) on child abuse, we considered the possibility that age categorisations within childhood reflect an adult-centric hierarchical ordering of knowledge. We therefore ignored age divisions and spoke with children across a range of ages.

The study

In asking children to contribute their perspectives on child abuse, we sought through collaboration with them, to break the silence 'created when those who are the subjects of the research have little or no power in the construction of accounts about them' (Lincoln 1993: 32). As adult researchers seeking to contribute to the child abuse discourse from the standpoint of children and young people, we responded to research with children in terms of the four criteria defined by Lincoln as 'imperatives' when researching the silenced (Lincoln 1993).

In response to the imperative of applying research strategies appropriate to researching with the silenced (Lincoln 1993), we adapted strategies already developed for researching the lives of other silenced groups. We were most familiar with qualitative methodology used in researching women's issues by exploring their understanding of these issues. In recent times there has been an increasing application of qualitative research methods to facilitate children contributing directly from their lived experiences. In using such research methods, children and young people interviewed are acknowledged as competent actors able to give plausible accounts of their worlds.

The focus of our study was on children in the mainstream population. Our strategies were designed to contribute to policies to improve the 'lived' lives of children, as they experience them while children. Our concern contrasted with those researchers on childhood who use traditional methodologies in studying abuse. The focus of these researchers on quantifying abuse and defining deviancy with the goals of promoting 'normative' childhood and functional adults, has excluded children as knowers.

In attending to Lincoln's second imperative, of hearing the perspectives of children and young people, we were attentive to methods for minimising discomfort in researching with a subjugated group. Katz (1995) has identified the way in which children's feelings of safety are increased when focus groups are formed from young people who already interact. We approached children we knew, or knew through other adults. These children then identified friends interested in participating. We considered the implications for gathering and interpreting the data of the fact that in many instances the participants had some degree of existing relationship with one or other of the researchers. The fact that in all instances the second researcher was not known to the participants was important in facilitating ongoing reflexivity in the research process.

All the young people chose to be interviewed in small groups, rather than individually. Groups were offered to the young people as a way of reducing power inequalities between the adult interviewers and young interviewees. There is increasing recognition of the value of focus groups, in contrast with individual interviews in researching with children, as a method of diluting the asymmetrical power relationship between adult researcher and child research participants (Beresford 1997; Katz 1995).

A total of thirteen young persons participated in the project. The participants were aged between 11 and 17 and were girls and boys from both state and private schools and from a range of cultural backgrounds. The older young people applied the word 'kids' to themselves and saw themselves as being children or non-adults, by virtue of their exclusion from the adult world. The size of the groups varied between two and four research participants. There was one group of four girls and the other three groups included both girl and boy participants.

In facilitating the collaborative process of the research, the children played the major role in determining not only the composition of their focus group, but also when and where the interviews took place, the method of recording and whether reporting back was appropriate. All the interviews were held in private homes, the younger participants preferring to sit around a table, whilst the older chose the living room chairs or floor. All the participants agreed to be taped and they managed the tape recorder. The interviews lasted between one and two and a half hours.

The university ethics committee determined we obtain, in addition to the consent of the children themselves, parental consent before the children and young people participated. In order to recognise the young people as actors with autonomy, we asked them, once they had consented to participate, to present the forms to their parents for their consent. A number of other young people interested in participating in the research could not obtain the consent of their parents and were therefore excluded. In the context of research around what children consider child abuse, this process raised for us similar questions to those discussed in research on a related topic (Hood, Kelley and Mayall 1996), about the role of adults in gatekeeping the participation of children.

In the focus interviews, which comprised the data collection methods of this project, we asked children and young people to discuss what they understood child abuse to be and how they would describe child abuse. Our responsibility as researchers was to facilitate and enable discussion. This involved introducing the topic and explaining how as researchers both working and researching in the area of child abuse, we had realised that although children were the people at the centre of concern of policies on child abuse, they had rarely been asked what they thought abuse was. Instead, child abuse had been defined by adults. We told the participants that we were asking a number of young people for their opinions.

The children all started the discussion with what they understood to be the accepted definition of abuse. They then continued by giving their own perspectives. In the discussion process the young people talked between themselves about what they considered abusive. We came into the discussion to clarify the points being made. If, as occasionally occurred, we had understood something different from what they were trying to say the children corrected us. Some of the group discussions were more free-flowing than others, with some young people appearing more articulate. The young people in talk amongst themselves tended to reach consensus on many issues.

Our second area of responsibility as researchers was 'faithfully' to convey the responses of the children and young people interviewed (Lincoln 1993). Because children and young people lack access to research and policy forums and rely on adults to convey their standpoint, we were concerned to collect and present their data in a way which would redress previous research imbalances. The participants told us they were not interested in us reporting back to them, for their comment, our interpretation of the data. This suggested either that these young people lacked a sense that they owned knowledge, which could be based on their previous experiences of exclusion from knowledge production, or that they experienced written data as abstracted from their knowledge or experience. Stainton-Rogers and Stainton-Rogers (1992) refer to the way children's knowledge is generally only published once it has been edited or interpreted by educators and other adults. Another possibility is that the children had simply moved on to other things by the time we were ready to submit the data to them.

We assumed a third area of responsibility: to reproduce texts which would represent the standpoint of the children and young people in a way which would be understandable and relevant to policy makers and practitioners promoting the interests of children and young people. In pursuing this criterion we analysed the data obtained in the research around themes and patterns of themes and linked these to existing discourses on child abuse.

Fourthly, in conducting the research we attempted to mitigate against any potential harm to children arising from the research. As researchers on the topic of abuse we were very aware of our duty of care to the young people who participated in the research. Although we planned that the discussion would be general rather than specific, the free-flowing nature of the conversation meant that it was possible that a disclosure of information that was troubling to a young person could have arisen. Being experienced in working with children and with child abuse, we had the skills to deal with a disclosure had it occurred. Contact numbers for organisations such as *The Kids Help Line* were given to the young people as well as invitations to contact the researchers at any time.

Feedback from the young people following the groups was very positive. Many expressed pleasure at having had an opportunity to have a say.

In presenting data from and discussion on this project, all names referred to are pseudonyms.

Children's definitions of abuse

Presentation of data analysis

The emergent themes from the data are presented below. As two adult researchers attempting to convey our understanding of the children's discourse on abuse as faithfully as possible, we have included many quotes from the children. These quotes illustrate the data which influenced our explication of each of the themes.

The emotional context of interpersonal relationships

In responding to the question of what they considered as child abuse, the children did not generally focus on specific physical actions, but on the structure of adult/child relations, and the way in which this provided a context for emotional hurt. Although specific actions of 'smacking' and 'swearing' at children are identified as abusive, the emphasis in discussions was not on physical harm *per se* as abusive, but on the emotional context of the emotional hurt which accompanied the physical actions.

'I think physical hurt is um also mentally.' (Sarah)

'The physical abuse contributes to the emotional abuse and the sexual abuse contributes to the emotional.' (Wendy)

'. . . kind of like someone getting to you from your insides, like shredding something that really matters to you.' (Sarah)

Significant are the consequent 'emotional scars (because) they last forever'. (Jack)

Children's emotions have received little attention in the social science literature generally and in the child abuse literature, specifically. Typically, where children's emotions are taken into consideration it is in terms of concepts such as bonding and attachment. Applying such concepts to the emotional experiences of children, while useful at a level of generalisation, ignores and objectifies the meaning these experiences have for individuals at specific times. The meanings that emerge from these children's discussions of the emotional context of abuse are related to their expectations of support from adults with whom they are in relationships.

'. . . it's worse if it's someone you thought you trusted . . . . just to think you trust someone and think they're there for you and then suddenly they're not. Suddenly they're totally turning against you, it's a really big shock.' (Sarah)

'. . . because your parents are so nice to you all the time, usually'. (Dan)

What is significant in all experiences of abuse is that it feels 'like they don't really care'. (Stefan)

'. . . like there's no-one there for you . . . When you are alone you don't have anyone to back you up.' (Sarah)

Legitimised inequality in adult-child relations

The children relate their vulnerability to having their feelings hurt to the unequal power relationships between children and adults. These inequalities mean that adults are able to respond to children with physical, behavioural and emotional actions, in ways that are denied to children. All the interactions which the children and young people describe as abusive, can be characterised as situations where children are positioned structurally, so that they have no leverage for negotiation. This is most evident in terms of adult physical actions towards children.

The children consider physical actions such as smacking abusive because they are experienced as related to their subjugated positioning as children.

'Because you're not allowed to smack anyone else but children . . . I can't smack.' (Jack)

'Because you can't do anything back.' (Marie)

A discussion in one group commenced with a description of child abuse in somewhat conventional terms and then explained it in terms of parent/child power issues.

Interviewer: So what do you think child abuse is?
Ian: It's like the way that an adult treats a kid. Could be a kid to a kid. But like, it's mainly the parents. I reckon that, just say the kid does something wrong, or maybe the Mum and Dad comes back home drunk, or has a very bad day and they blame it on the kids. By like hitting them and stuff like that. But sometimes it's because they think they have power over kids, so they can treat them however they want.
Interviewer: They think they've got power over kids?
Ian: Yeah. Sort of like, it's my kid, I can do whatever I want with them.

Physical punishment has historically been a legitimated part of unequal relationships, imposed by persons in positions of authority on others subordinate to them. It has been inherent in master-slave, husband-wife and master-apprentice relations. The application of the concept of human rights has, in contemporary times, eroded the legitimacy of these unequal relations and the use of physical punishment within them. As Leach states 'we have universal human rights now – universal except for children, that is' (1994: 126). It is the treatment of children as not fully human:

'as less of a person' (Anne)

which these children were identifying as the significant part of adult behaviour to children, which they defined as abusive.

'You're just a kid you don't count . . . you're not one of us.' (Julie)

'. . . always patronising kind of thing'. (Anne)

In one group discussion the children identified adult attitudes of discounting children as linked with stereotyping and prejudice.

Julie:	Some adults I find are like prejudiced against kids, like they just treat all of us like as teenagers . . . ah dyed hair, get away from me
Sarah:	Yeah like that, because my next door neighbour hates me, you guys know that (Laughter);
Interviewer:	Is that a sign of abuse, if we hate kids?
Julie:	Yeah, I think it is, like giving off a really bad vibe, that they hate us and that's like abusive because they're saying, oh we don't like you because
Interviewer:	and it's
Louise:	Yeah and um when I, at my concert last year, me and my friend we went to buy some flowers for our teachers and we walked past this bus stop and there were some people and this lady there, she started hitting us with her umbrella, saying you don't belong here, piss off, no children should be here, just piss off and get away from here, you don't belong here and she was hitting us with her umbrella.

The children consider themselves discriminated against on the basis of a hierarchy of age. So that while:

'. . . the majority of (young) people are crying out for a say' (Dan)

being a child or young person means you are not taken seriously:

'You have no opinions . . .' (Sarah)

'You're not old enough to choose (your religion). You don't have the knowledge or anything.' (Mandy)

'We're similar to a minority group, but we don't get as many rights. Before Aboriginal people couldn't vote or couldn't go into pub or do all that sort of stuff. We can't vote, we can't go into pubs, we can't do that. Not that we necessarily want to do that, but we have some of the same restrictions that have been given to minority groups.' (Jack)

Child abuse is identified as significant in maintaining the power of the adult administering the punishment to subjugate the child.

'Like the person hitting you had more power or something. It's about power and they're making others feel powerless against them.' (Ian)

'Well I kinda think abuse also has something to do with power, like in my family my dad used to do the wooden spoon thing, and so I think he used to feel that he had to be powerful because he was like the man of the house, and um he kind of felt that he had to be powerful so he had a problem so he had to do something, so that's how he did it.' (Sarah)

In the *private domestic arena* they describe abuse as based on power implicit in the parental role.
    There is a feeling that:

'. . . we're all oppressed by our parents'. (Jack)

Some of this oppression within the family is through emotional bonds:

'Like the family has also like, another certain injection of control. If you're abused by, say, a family friend you're not going to tell your family because it'll hurt them too much, so you don't – don't tell anyone. You don't want to hurt them primarily.' (Mandy)

In one group there was a discussion of how power wielded through emotional attachments contributes to abuse by family members:

Mandy: But I mean, it's the truth that the family has far more power than any child
Interviewer: Who has?
Mandy: The family
Interviewer: Yes?
Mandy: Than anything else. Like, not even like power, like, by saying like, saying their power. Like saying no, no, no. You can't do this. But just emotionally, you're bound to the people where you feel you can't wrong them and that.
Interviewer: So does that make it more possible for parents to abuse?
Mandy: Yeah

Interviewer.   And this emotional binding, is it emotional binding? Is it dependency?

Jack: It starts off as dependency. But then the parents just can't let go.

There is the sense of the family controls being internalised in Mandy's response to the family's emotional needs.

> 'Don't you still feel emotionally bound by your parents like, trying to do the best you can for them?' (Mandy)

The notion of control and its relationship to power is extended to the *public arena:*

> 'Everyone that has control abuses it, just about . . . teachers, parking inspectors . . . the police, the schools, the society.' (Jack)

The children explicitly associate adult attempts to control children, with adult concern that undisciplined children might be dangerous to the maintenance of the social order.

> 'They're dangerous . . . whenever she's talking about teenagers that she's never met before (in contrast to her grandchildren and their friends), they're always really awful, young, naughty little boys and girls.' (Jack)

> 'My mum and dad got so worried (about sister) . . . they used to be so scared of her, because she'd go wild . . . everyone would get angry at her.' (Julie)

Adults are seen to be attempting to control children by establishing boundaries limiting their use of public places:

> 'Like if you have a large group and a small group, the small group feel threatened and more into like show that they have more power. . . . It's kind of like, . . . it's like, old people are there . . . and there's a lot of teenagers around them, then they're going to go; Oh, they're awful. Because they're scared. And they go . . . take up their two seats (in the bus) – put their boundaries up.' (Mandy)

Autonomy and resistance

That some children have power to resist and challenge adult control is suggested by the comment of one child:

> 'I was a strong child and so I used that to control people to do the things that I wanted them to do.' (Julie)

More generally, these children express feelings about adults including those with whom they have relationships, not hearing them. This is relevant to their apprehensiveness about disclosing abuse. They see the consequences of such disclosures being fear of further emotional hurt within families, and distrust of being able to influence decisions about them at the public decision making level.

For this reason, they are sceptical about disclosing abuse to a public authority:

> 'If the individual themself wants to raise something about it. Then yeah good on them. But I think that not all that many . . . I'm pretty sure the majority of people that have undergone some type of abuse probably don't do anything about it, solely because of this control thing, messing with a higher power, you're not going to bother trying to, you think you've got no . . . (control).' (Jack)

Here the children exhibited a sense of agency:

> 'Because think about it. Would you rather be hit once a week, with your parents, or (be) somewhere else and not (hit). Easy choice . . . being emo- tionally torn apart every second of every day because they've taken you away from your family, compared to being beaten, moderately lightly, maybe once a week. I don't think it's even a comparison.' (Dan)

The children's agency was limited by their emotional and structural dependency:

> '. . . you and your parents have been like together and they support you and if you, if maybe you go against them then they'll go against you and you've got no-one to support you.' (Sarah)

> 'So much relies on other people's decision for you – like even when you make the decision for yourself it's still got through somewhere else.' (Dan)

Children's limited agency in situations where relationships with the adult deci- sion makers are not emotionally positive is of particular concern to them:

> 'The funny thing is that these people get to work for us, like do you know what I mean, like these people who hate children get to work for us but we don't even get a say.' (Julie)

The children believe their opportunities for agency should be extended. They desire participation on the basis of equality. This includes having money and being able to vote:

> 'I heaps wanted to vote when I was little.' (Mandy)

Basically:

'What kids want is to be treated equally. . . .' (Julie)

and to have the opportunity to negotiate:

'. . . like I would like to be able to have a two-way compromise'. (Julie)

Discussion

In examining the extent and depth of discussions and resultant contributions of the participants, we found neither gender nor age to be relevant. Educational background may have influenced the ability to articulate ideas. More influential was the degree of comfort individuals felt in the group as determined by relationships within their groups. One young person commented in relation to her attitude to discussing the topic of abuse 'we're really good friends and I'm more comfortable' talking with members of this group than would have been the case with other possible groupings of friends.

The children who contributed to this research had not, to the researchers' knowledge, been formally identified as abused. Therefore, it could be argued that their discussion on abuse reflected a lack of knowledge of what the official discourse describes as child abuse. We however understood that they were likely, like most children in our society, to have been exposed to a wide range of information about child abuse, most of it within the dominant discourse. Most claimed to have had special classroom sessions on child abuse, which they discounted as not very useful or memorable. Much of the information on child abuse available to them would have been that available to adults, in the media and in particular in television serials targeted at young people (such as *Neighbours* and *Heartbreak High*).

Analysis of the data obtained in discussions with the children participating in this research, identified abuse as the use of power to control children. This control is exercised through physical actions, emotional constraints and boundary-setting which devalues and excludes younger people from adult, or mainstream society. From the standpoint of the children who contributed to this research, children are abused by adults as a consequence of their positioning in the generational order. (For further discussion of children's views on adult power see also Chapter 9.)

The findings in our research that 'all families oppress their children' challenges the concept of abuse being about some pathological families whose deviancy can be treated and thereby the problem of child abuse solved. This analysis of abuse from the standpoint of children extends our understanding of the nature of child abuse beyond that provided by the dominant adultist discourse on child abuse. The dominant discourse in responding to abuse in terms of 'a specific group of children' being 'at risk' pathologises the behaviour of some parents.

That these children and parents tend to be in families disadvantaged in terms of gender, class and race (Mason 1993; Thorpe 1994) highlights the way in which policies based on the dominant discourse, by individualising and pathologising some individuals in marginalised families, reinforce a concept of normative families. As a consequence the patriarchal family as an institution is bolstered rather than threatened (Mason and Noble-Spruell 1993; Makrinotti 1994).

The analysis of the children's definition of abuse accords with the findings of those writers who have challenged the construction of child abuse and exploitation as abnormal or dysfunctional behaviour, understanding abuse and exploitation as more extreme expressions of prevailing social relationships between children and adults (Ennew 1994; Waksler 1996). The young people who participated in this research describe abuse as institutionalised in society, through the legitimation of hierarchical authority on the basis of age differences which serve as the rationale for discriminating between adults and non-adults: that is children.

The young people experienced structural inequality as a devaluing and excluding of them as non-adults from participation in society. The construction of childhood as a period of exclusion from adult society, in conjunction with the familialisation of childhood which ensures dependency within the family, precludes children's agency in abusive situations. The lack of possibility of agency for children and young people contrasts with other oppressed groups and is reflected in the comment 'we're similar to a minority group, but we don't get as many rights'. The difference between women and children in relation to possibilities for agency has been noted by some researchers (e.g. Otter 1986; Gordon 1989). They have drawn attention to the fact that children lack the agency available to women to counter violence: either individually, through seeking divorce from violent partners; through the actions of other women, as in the opening of refuges; or with other women, politically through the vote.

The exercise of 'choice' by young people in this research, given abusive interactions in the family, to remain in the family rather than seek agency assistance, assumes a significance which can partly be understood in terms of research by Hood et al. (1996). They found that in the home, in contrast with the social agency of the school, adult control is balanced by caring. Implicit within this discussion on emotional hurt and the choices available to them for dealing with abuse, was an attitude of the young people that their parents did 'care' about them, and that this provided some, even if limited, leverage for negotiation and agency on the child's part. The lack of similar relationships in young people's interactions with adult-centred public agencies, exacerbates the inherent power imbalances and contributes to what has been described as children's 'uniquely disadvantaged negotiating position' in dealing with social agencies (Mayall 1996: 83).

Of major significance for understanding the ineffectiveness of the state in dealing with child abuse, is the extent to which children interpreted their structural positioning as abuse. Public agency child protection practice in reinforcing, rather than challenging the asymmetry between adults and children (MacKinnon 1998; Chisholm 1979) denies children the agency and opportunities to negotiate their own positioning in social relations – the basis to abuse in the private arena of the family. The construction of children as either subservient or threatening denies them the opportunity to confront abusive situations and reduces the likelihood of any redistribution of power from adults to younger people both within and outside the family.

Acknowledgements

We express our appreciation to the young people who generously contributed their time and thoughts to the data which forms the basis for this chapter.

Some of the data reproduced in this chapter have been used as the basis of another paper, directed at a practitioner readership in Australia.

9 Understanding childhoods: a London study

Berry Mayall

Introduction: contexts for enquiry

This chapter explores children's discourse about childhood, in relation to motherhood, fatherhood and child-parent relationships. A key concept guiding this enquiry is the observation that 'child' has to be understood as a relational concept (Aries 1972). We can distinguish at least three sets of relationships. Children are those identified by adults as non-adults, so the social world that adults construct consists of two groups with somewhat separate interests and relationships to the social order. Secondly, children's lives are structured by adults – by their interests, understandings and goals; the social condition of childhood is defined through adult-child relations mediated through these interests, understandings and goals. Thirdly, the family and to a lesser extent the school operates on the basis of personal including affective relationships between adults and children. Thus, the permanent social category childhood can be seen as structured in relation to adulthood.

Of specific interest and usefulness in studying child-adult relations is the concept of generation (see Chapter 2). This throws emphasis on how social forces shape the experiences and understandings of groups of people, which in turn contribute to the character of those child-adult relations (Mannheim 1952 [1928]). The childhoods of today's children may be seen as shaped by a different constellation of forces compared with those that shaped their parents' and teachers' childhoods; yet parents and teachers are currently operating in intersection with the same constellation of forces that impinge on their children. Child-adult relations are therefore structured and operationalised at the intersections of the understandings derived (in part) from social influences, that individuals and groups work with. Education policy in the UK provides an example here. Parents and teachers grew up under the influences of policies current in the 1970s (and deriving from those of the 1960s), but both they and children are now faced with dramatic changes in education policies, formulated in the late 1980s.

The concept of generation is thus useful in drawing attention to people in their membership of groups, and to how group experience and understanding is shaped by large-scale historically rooted influences, ideologies and policies.

In the case of children this is especially useful in helping us to become more sociological, to move from a focus on the individual child and local adult influences on her, and to lift children and childhood, theoretically speaking, out of the family. Then we can begin to see children as a social group operating in relation to the social order; to understand local activities and interactions in relation to large-scale forces.

Key to understanding the character of childhood at any given point is the dominant social understanding of the appropriate balance of responsibility for childhood, as between the parents and the state. It can be argued that societies conduct a continuous negotiation about this division of responsibility (Shamgar-Handelman 1994). Wintersberger (1996) argues that attention to children's protection and provision rights is a pre-condition of assuring their participation rights; countries vary in how far they have seriously addressed the appropriate issues, but probably in all countries radical and concerted changes are needed to the material conditions of daily life (such as child-friendly town planning), and in the distribution of parents' working time. It seems that even in countries such as Sweden, where public rhetoric has been somewhat matched by public policy towards partnership between state and parents to assure children's rights, social and economic pressures devalue those rights (Björnberg 1996).

The specifically UK version of generational relations tilts the balance of responsibility for child welfare heavily towards parents – mainly to mothers; and in the 1990s this emphasis became particularly marked. Currently, parental responsibility is not well matched even at the level of public rhetoric with societal, or state responsibility for children and for childhood. A key example is that parents are considered responsible for keeping their children safe; societal responsibility for making environments safe comes a very bad second. 'Traffic danger' and 'stranger danger' act as powerful structures conditioning how parents and children live their daily lives. Hillman, Adams and Whitelegg (1990) have documented the disappearance of children from public places. Many 9 year olds are accompanied to and from school by parents, and children's access unescorted to streets, parks and other local facilities is restricted or denied by parents, and hedged about with rules. Parents (and children) regard few spaces as safe and children must each time ask permission to go out, say where they are going, with whom, and be back at a certain time (Kelley, Mayall and Hood 1997). (See Chapter 10 for a different balance between state and parental responsibility for children.)

Just as public spaces are organised in the interests of adults, so too is the second major space and time where children's days are spent: the school. In recent years, developing UK government education policies, through a national curriculum, regular testing and the encouragement of competitiveness between schools, have, with increasing overtness, defined children as the objects rather than the subjects of education (for discussion see Triggs and Pollard 1998; Conner 1998); policy is overwhelmingly concerned with their future economic usefulness rather than their active learning experiences. (But see Chapter 6 for children's 'time-shifting' tactics.) Thus, at school, as in public places, children have little ability to determine how they spend their time. As dependants in child-adult relations, they are not visible as moral decision-makers, and not conceptualised as such.

The third main setting where children spend time, the home, is the site of complex ideologies on parent-child relations. Current rhetoric proposing democratic relationships is undermined in the UK by dominant developmental concepts, which stress inequalities of knowledge and competence; and these discourses underplay power issues, notably social pressures on mothers to fit their children for their future lives in a society riven by gender and social class divisions (Walkerdine and Lucey 1989: Chapter 1). In the light of this point, we must be cautious in interpreting recent data, from mothers (Brannen et al. 1994; Mayall 1994a; Ribbens 1994) who say they value their children's rights to make decisions on issues that concern them at home, and to participate in family decision-making. Some evidence from children's own accounts indicates that they think their participation rights are routinely brushed aside (e.g. Thomas and O'Kane 1999).

In considering the specific contexts for children's lives – and the children discussed here live in London – it is also relevant to take account of the diversity of families, along three main intersecting dimensions: household composition, ethnicity and household income. National data give us pictures which are played out in extreme forms in the cities. A third of children will experience change in which parents live with them; about 20 per cent of children at any one time live with one parent (National Stepfamily Association 1998). In the UK, and especially in the cities, live people whose roots, back one, two or more generations, are in many countries, and especially countries previously under British domination (some African countries, the West Indies, India, Pakistan and Bangladesh); London is the most common first destination for refugees. By the early 1990s, child poverty rates had soared to 31 per cent; single-parent families and some ethnic minority families are particularly highly represented in this group (Wilkinson 1994).

An empirical study – 'Negotiating Childhoods'

In this study I set out to explore empirically with young people their understandings of what it is to be a child or to be called a child and how they experience and interpret their own daily lives. From a theoretical point of view, the main aim was to consider how their accounts resonate with normative and sociological understandings of the social condition of childhood. How do sociological concepts help us understand what children say? Can we begin to move towards a child standpoint as a basis for understanding their social positioning?

'Negotiating Childhoods' ran formally for two years (September 1997 to August 1999)[1]. It is a small-scale exploratory study which seeks information from young people on their understandings and experiences of childhood. I collected data with 9–10 and 12–13 year olds. In this paper I focus on fifty-seven 9–10 year olds, based in two primary Year 5 classes in East and North London schools.

On terminology, I note here that whilst the older group had mixed views on whether they felt themselves to be children or teenagers or students, the younger group – those under discussion in this chapter – were all quite clear that not only were they designated as children, but that they felt themselves to be children. In this chapter I use the term children.

Though I did not aim to establish detailed demographic facts about their families, it was clear from their accounts that they formed a multi-ethnic sample, reflecting the history of immigration into London. The sample included children with West Indian and European backgrounds and with ethnically mixed backgrounds; twenty-five of the twenty-eight children in East School had parents who had immigrated from the Indian sub-continent. Judging by their accounts of their parents' work and their housing, a minority of the fifty-seven children (about nine, all in North School) were from 'middle-class' homes. Their accounts of their own and their parents' daily life also indicate that many parents were struggling to provide for their families; in nine families there was no-one earning and in others, the jobs were of kinds characterised by long hours and low pay; some professional-class parents were also working long hours. In all, forty-three of the fifty-seven children lived in two-parent families, including twenty-six of the twenty-eight East children; and seventeen of the twenty-nine North children.

The research was designed as a process; I spent a day a week with each class over 6–8 weeks. I acted as general helper around the classroom, so that we all had a chance to get to know each other, ate lunch with the children, and hung around the playground. I sought consent from the children at the outset and also with reference to each proposed session. (Every child wanted to take part.) I worked first with pairs of children, asking them to discuss childhood and parenthood; and then interviewed children individually about their daily life. I collected some simple factual data through questionnaires. Then groups of four or five discussed the merits and demerits of school. In whole class sessions I related my understandings of what they had said for further discussion. For each class, I drafted a book for the children – consisting mainly of quotations grouped under topics, and discussed and developed the draft with them before amending it and giving them each a copy.

So the data consist mainly of transcripts of conversations with the children. These conversations were collected in a specific context, the school, and in the even more specific context that we left the classroom for a quiet room or corner where we could spend half an hour or so. I was probably an unusual figure in the children's experience: an adult stranger, older than their teachers and parents, asking for detailed information about childhood, and providing time for children to talk at length about themselves and their families. I tried to mitigate any strangeness by working towards a protective social environment for these conversations. The children chose a companion for the pair session and I encouraged them to discuss points with each other. By the time of the individual interviews, children knew me quite well, had talked with me in pairs and in most cases seemed at ease; again, within broad topics, I aimed to let the child develop and diverge as appropriate. The group discussions about school were the least directed, most informal of the sessions: the children joked and swapped stories, agreed and disagreed with each other, added points and diverted the conversation at will. Overall, then, the social context of data collection was that of interested adult requesting children's help in understanding childhood; it was formal, in that there was a one-page topic list as a guide. But to some extent the sessions followed their agenda since, firstly, most of them seemed to like talking about themselves and understood the session as a suitable occasion to do so; and secondly, the format allowed them to direct or divert the conversation somewhat as they wished.

Childhood and parenthood compared

In the opening paired discussions, the central aim was to explore the generational relationships understood and experienced by children. First I asked them to reflect directly on the social characteristics and status of motherhood, fatherhood and childhood, through such topics as: What is it like being a mother/father/child? What are the good things? And any bad things? This was an attempt to explore their ideas in general about these social statuses, before homing in on their experiences of generational issues.

There are potential problems in this approach. By focusing on social categories and general descriptions I might be encouraging stereotyping of, for instance, childhood. In practice, however, children moved easily back and forth between normative and experiential accounts, and this formed a useful contrast – as I discuss below.

Children's initial (normative?) accounts of parenthood were based on clear gendered divisions of responsibility. Fathers have responsibility for the financial welfare of the family, and mothers for childcare and home maintenance. Parenthood is 'hard', and motherhood especially 'hard', partly because the responsibilities are inescapable and because of the many, unending tasks, some of which conflict. Some mothers also carry responsibility for financing the family, where there is no father, or no father who earns enough, or where mothers wish to do paid work.

When they then went on to talk about childhood – still, initially in general terms – their comments referred to clear contrasts with parenthood and adulthood. Children differ from adults and especially from parents, since they do not carry serious or ultimate responsibilities; children are subordinate to parents, must obey them, and must learn morality from them. Whereas adults must take responsibility for themselves and for others, the status of childhood is such that children should be able to assume they will be protected and provided for. Childhood lacks the rights of adulthood: children cannot enter pubs or drive cars, or 'do what you like'. But children have the right to have fun and free time.

These comments were remarkably consistent across both sexes and the range of socio-economic and ethnic backgrounds. Their comments may be interpreted as normative, as deriving from general societal understandings, mediated through parental and media discourse, about the proper character of the three social positions. But in addition, children might be extrapolating from their own experience and from their knowledge of other children's childhoods and family relationships. It was therefore interesting to hear from them about their daily lives and the important issues they identified as arising from events and relationships. I thought, and so it proved, that the normative accounts of these social positions would not square entirely with children's experience.

In all homes except one, where the mother had died, children described their mothers as carrying the main responsibility and work of childcare and control. In general, she was at home, more than fathers; the accounts of daily life included reference to far more conversations with mothers than with fathers. For most children she was the principal person they discussed issues with and sought help from. Children described mothers' stressful days: combining paid work, childcare and housework; the specific tasks of looking after younger children as well as other tasks; problems of managing older children; problems in their own personal relationships.

Children's accounts indicated much more mixed experience of fathers, both across and within 'cases'. A few fathers were reported as important in family and child-parent interactions. Some fathers were out long hours or even overnight at work; others were unemployed or retired. Some children identified their father as carrying moral responsibility for the family, others that fathers had abandoned that responsibility. Some commented that, unlike the mother, their father regarded the home as his leisure space and time. In 26 per cent of cases (two in East and twelve in North schools), children's fathers lived elsewhere and in some cases had been replaced by 'Mum's boy-friend' or 'stepdad'. Notably, where there had been these challenges to normative concepts of the two-parent family, or where their mother did not conform to the mother-as-housewife model, children tended to discuss parents and family life in great detail. Children also commented adversely on deviations from family norms: parents should not be out at work till all hours, but should 'be there for' their children. Those whose parents had split up discussed their participation in conversations with parents about the past, present and future of the situation; and their continued attempts at contact with the non-resident parent. (By contrast with the 12 year olds, many of these children were currently experiencing processes and transitions in family living arrangements and in contact arrangements.)

The social status of childhood was, in their accounts of daily life, clearly distinguished from adulthood. This was expressed in points the children made about dependency, responsibility, free time and apprenticeship. The general point – that they are dependent on their parents for provision and protection – was substantiated through their accounts of access to resources. Children had money only if received as pocket money – either earned, or given automatically, or given with supplements for work done or for being good. Children's access to local services and facilities – parks, clubs, shops, playgrounds, cinemas – depended on parental willingness to give permission, to pay and in most cases to escort. In all cases, their parents allowed them out only with provisos – where, when and with whom; and most children described asking permission as a continual feature of daily life. Their accounts also show that their access to public space was very limited geographically – to the route to school and the nearest shop, the pavement outside the house, the play area on the estate. Some were not allowed 'out' at all. Thus in general children's access to social intercourse outside the home was mediated through parents.

Interesting discussions took place around the linked themes of free time and jobs. The notion of children's dependency as people who are provided for contextualised their accounts of jobs around the home. Almost all the children did some housework and many looked after younger siblings; but most did not present these activities as responsibilities, but rather as delegated tasks. Indeed the attempt to opt out of jobs was often described in terms of how childhood is meant to be lived: their right to free time, for doing what they chose, for fun, and for being with friends (see also Chapter 3).

The apprenticeship theme ran through every child's accounts, though with varying emphases (see next section). In general, children accepted their minority position, as people who know less than adults, and must learn from them; school was an important site for learning what you need for jobs and careers, home was the principal source of learning about morality. On the question whether children did any work, there was a range of views. Many initially said no. When I raised the issue of school, some children then argued that their school-related activity came under the heading apprenticeship; it was not work, because it was for your own future benefit. However, some children claimed that their activity at school and their homework was work, because you had to do it, and it was hard. A complementary theme here was that work was activity undertaken in order to provide for the family's welfare; so housework but not school-related activity was work. Work was also activity that is paid for.

Negotiating childhoods?

The above points will be discussed next in more detail, in the light of emphasis within the 'new childhood studies' on children as agents negotiating their childhoods. As sociological researchers we have been learning to move from the child as object of socialisation to children as agents in the project of their own lives. But behind the term 'negotiation' lie some important assumptions. One source of its assumed importance is debates about structure and agency. These suggest relationships between people and between people and structures in terms of movement towards goals. The idea of negotiation commonly includes a notion of process whereby a person aims to arrive at change beneficial to him or her. Within the conceptual frameworks of structure-agency debates, therefore, there is a notion that people seek improvement, whether as individuals – for instance, a patient seeking better medical treatment, or an employee wanting a higher salary; or as a social group – for instance black people or women. In an earlier study, I myself identified the concept of a continuously re-negotiated contract as a feature of children's relationships with their parents; children's and parents' accounts suggested that children seek to acquire greater autonomy through re-siting the boundaries, challenging parental edicts, seizing control (Mayall 1994a).

Indeed, underlying the arguments about agency in sociological literature is a range of assumptions and/or concepts deriving from Western European cultural traditions. Thus within the structures of modernity, it is assumed that we want progress – society and individuals do and should seek to change for the better (Therborn 1995, Chapter 1). Value is placed on individual enterprise and achievement. Challenges to the status quo are to be admired, if they are accompanied by suggestions for improvement; and problem-solvers are therefore highly valued (for discussion from a feminist angle, see Grimshaw 1986).

The work I have done for the study under consideration here has forced me to consider the above points. I should like to draw attention to issues concerning the concept of socialisation, and to cultural variations and commonalities in outlook.

Children's accounts of what it is to be a child indicate both a range of views as between children, and more than one view from any one child. As I have described, children strongly voice their recognition of adult power and their mixed reactions to it, ranging from unquestioning acceptance, to tactical activities, to instances of resentful resistance. But overall, obedience and acceptance are commoner than resistance and rejection. Children say that they lack power, choice and autonomy, but that these are not components of the social status of childhood. The up-sides of childhood are protection and provision, freedom from responsibility, free time and opportunities for fun. Getting an education is also a good feature of childhood; a common, and virtually universal theme is that childhood is a time for learning what you need to know for later life; this is couched in terms of schooling, but in some cases children say they don't know enough yet to make good choices; and that since they do not have responsibility they therefore are not in a position to make choices. Thus children are proposing that learning culturally appropriate knowledge and morality is a central task with which they engage in childhood.

A specific slant on this approach to childhood was given me by seventeen Muslim children in the first class I worked in, at East School. They were very ready indeed with sentences in reply to my opening gambits: What is it like being a child? And what do parents expect of children? These children said: childhood is hard, but not as hard as parenthood; you have to work hard at school and at the mosque, and do jobs at home; you get some free time – but not enough and mainly at weekends. Children should be good, they should be obedient, work hard and be helpful at home. They should learn from their parents and from their religious teacher; it was acceptable for these adults to employ physical punishment as a sanction. These children had been taught these principles from their earliest days, and were virtually quoting from the Qu'ran. They were living lives almost totally structured by the demands of home, mosque and school; some had three lots of homework – from each set of adults. Learning the Qu'ran (for boys) and reading the Qu'ran or stories within Islamic tradition (for girls) was required by the mosque teacher; children must carry out these activities five days a week, at the mosque or at home (commoner for girls). In this particular school, too, teachers were putting great emphasis on the importance of homework in helping to advance the children's prospects. Apart from these demands, their social lives out of school were with a wide range of kin, living locally; some also attended language classes and sports sessions; all did some housework.

Their statements were impressive and consistent; they indicated clear understanding and acceptance of their position. Childhood was the period of life when you learned to be a good enough member of a cultural and religious group – at the levels of the family and of the wider community; and when you learned enough at school to get qualifications and a good job. These clearly understood beliefs gave solid structures to their lives; while a few, notably boys, indicated that they were over-pressured and over-controlled by adults, others, especially girls, expressed feelings of contentment, purpose and security within the beliefs and practices shaping their days.

The Muslim children's accounts provide at least three distinctive themes within the concept of 'negotiation': participation, self-formation and resistance. One theme is that they were learning how best to participate in Islamic religion and culture. Participation here means the individual activity of balancing what is desirable with what seems possible or acceptable. One should pray five times a day, but that was difficult – it involved getting up before dawn, and in school-time there was no opportunity for prayer. So as a person who wanted more sleep and who had to go to school, one compromised and settled for a modified best. Similarly, these children were deciding whether to fast for the month of Ramadan; this involves not eating or drinking between dawn and sunset. Children and parents discussed whether they should fast, given their age, weight, strength and willingness; some children said they decided, and others that parents decided for them and took the child's own view into account.

A second theme is that childhood is a time when you have the opportunity to shape yourself, and in this sense to engage in the project of your own life. Within the general Islamic framework of daily life and the longer-term expectations of 'being a good Muslim', and giving respect to parents over the life-span, children referred to a variety of goals, heavily influenced by parental wishes. It was clear that this generation of parents wanted their children to enter well-paid jobs, a desire we may understand in the specific context of major migration, poverty and a hard life in London. Boys described the advantages of being a chef or an engineer in terms of good pay, and the opportunity to rest. One boy was determined to become a Muslim teacher, and devoted large parts of the day to learning the Qu'ran, and to the practices of Islam. A girl, who came (as it seemed) from a liberal family, planned to go to university (her sisters had done so) and to follow family traditions by taking up a career as a teacher, though her own and her parents' plans were also for her to marry and have children; she saw her work at school as a means to higher education. Another girl, equally bright, strongly emphasised that a traditional woman's life was what she wanted: to do what her mother had done: get married, have children and spend her life at home; she was learning household tasks and Islamic ways of living in order to prepare herself for this future. So these children were shaping their daily lives somewhat in accordance with their proposed futures. As a first generation of Muslim children, born in the UK, they – and their parents – were dealing with and seeking accommodation between reproducing the Muslim community and taking advantage of opportunities for social and economic improvement.

A third theme in Muslim accounts was resistance. Children should have 'free time', but they didn't get enough of it. When I enquired why they should have free time, they said, adults get some free time, so children should too; or that, though adults did not have free time, children should have some, after their many tasks were accomplished. A context for this view was that life was hard, both in childhood and adulthood; people work hard, and they need rest. Notably, 'free time', rather than 'playtime' was the phrase they used. Free time meant time not under the immediate surveillance of adults; it was time when you chose your own activity. Since childhood was lived under the control and authority of adults, it was especially important for children to have some time they controlled themselves. These children told me of only short, fragmented patches of free time; commonly it consisted of about 15 minutes before leaving home for school, break times at school and up to half an hour after school before going to mosque. They described some resistances to adult demands. One boy went round to his cousins' house as often as possible to avoid tasks at home. Girls continued to read books or watch TV when their mother called to them to do housework. Boys asked to be allowed to play out in the street, and evaded requests to go shopping with their mothers (who were not allowed out on their own).

These three themes under the general heading 'negotiation' – participation, self-formation and resistance – provide food for thought regarding the other forty children. It seems to me that the general themes emerge, but with somewhat different faces. The theme of participation emerges clearly from their accounts of their activity in constructing the social order of the family; in this sense they negotiated a social position for themselves as a valued member of the family and learned the moral codes of the family through discussion. For instance, children took part in family life and special events, including religious festivities. Many girls and boys discussed with their mothers issues to do with, for instance, lone parenthood, their mother's new boy-friend, the birth of a new sibling, marital disputes, relatives' illnesses and deaths. Participatory activity also included household and family maintenance work; most children did a share of household work, running errands, looking after younger siblings; many kept up contacts with relatives, especially grandparents and non-resident fathers.

As to working on the project of one's own life, broadly the forty children had distinctive view-points, compared to the Muslim children. Most had no clear vision of what future life should or would hold, though some said their parents wanted them to 'stay on at school' or go to university. They did not cite specific jobs or careers to which they aimed. It seemed that the parents, compared to the Muslim parents, had less well defined ideas about their children's futures, or had not voiced them or had put less pressure on children to follow certain paths; and that children had a more open-ended vision of their futures. A few girls discussed the pros and cons of motherhood, as a possible, rather than inevitable or normal feature of their futures. But working on the project of one's own life had a distinctive time-present facet. Without additional homework from parents, mosque and language classes, these children had more time out of school to follow their own interests: at home, and through clubs, sporting activities, playtime with friends, some local shopping, television. A few said all their time was free out of school time, to read, use the computer, play, visit friends.

The third theme – resistance – also had a distinctive character. It was apparent that the less prescriptive character of home-life (compared to that of the Muslim children) allowed for discussion, argument, conflict and decision-making. The point alluded to earlier holds for the general population of the children; they reported negotiations about the 'contract' at home – principally about their use of free time. Some children thought some parental controls were somewhat unacceptable (though 'for their own good'). An interesting kind of resistance was to parental work-hours and timetables; several children resented the fact that their parents were 'always' out at work, and that they did not see them enough; children contrasted the ideal (a parent – usually a mother – at home 'for you') with the actuality (stressed over-worked parents).

The moral status of childhood

Underlying children's accounts of child-adult relationships are varying understandings of children's moral status. In order to consider this topic, I go back directly to the points adumbrated at the outset. Generational forces, I suggested, imply that children as a social group have a distinctive set of relations to the social order; that adults play a critical part in ordering children's lives; and that care and control relationships between parents and their children are a central context for defining and redefining children's social and moral character.

Children's inferior moral status – and more specifically the ascription of moral incompetence – is perhaps the principal focus for their designation as other than adults. Competence, as Alderson (1993: 32) discusses and demonstrates, currently has a double meaning: wisdom to know the correct decision, and courage to make a best guess and to take responsibility for it. Whilst these are contradictory, both are integral to modern meanings of competence. She uses the case of children facing critical surgery to explore their participation in decision-making, in partnership with parents and medical and nursing staff. Competence thus emerges, not as a capacity linked to developmental stage, but as context-related and developed through thought, feeling and action on events and relationships in the here-and-now (Hutchby and Moran-Ellis 1998a: 16). To the extent that children are denied the opportunity to exercise competence, they are likely to be less competent and through processes of mutual reinforcement they are especially likely to be regarded as lacking in competence.

Children in my study spoke directly about the ambivalent ways in which their moral status was defined and assigned in their daily lives. On the one hand, they found that they were assigned morally inferior status compared to parents, and they agreed with this; it was right that parents should teach them how to behave well, and should employ sanctions to make sure they learned. Some children explained that they were indeed morally unreliable, using various tactics to manage their lives, such as concealing the truth, pretending not to hear commands, playing on their mother's good mood to 'twist her arm'. This is a common theme in children's accounts (see especially Chapters 3, 5 and 6). It is, of course, the powerless who have to employ such deceitful tactics to reach a reasonably acceptable compromise within their inferior social status. On the other hand, in tandem with their assigned inferior moral status, children's accounts show that they were constantly expected to behave well. Accounts of parental and teacher anger about children's transgressions reflected this expectation. Some of this adult reaction was of the 'You're old enough to know better' type, and thereby squares with socialisation theory based on concepts of developmental stages. But some adult expectations of child behaviour 'now' derived from the requirement that children fit in with, or subordinate themselves to adult agendas. It was children's deviations from adult requirements which called forth conflict and rebuke. This was, of course, most obvious at school, where, to take a common example, the requirement to be quiet in class resulted from teacher-led schooling (rather than child-led learning). But children also gave examples from home life, where, for instance, their own wishes – to stay at home and watch TV or play with friends – had to give way to parental insistence that they take part in a shopping expedition. A good child accompanied his mother without making a fuss; resistance could lead to blame.

But children's stories also showed there was incompatibility between the assigned incompetence and their competence in practice: for their accounts demonstrate that they did carry out moral work, in maintaining and constructing relationships. Thus children comforted parents, showed tolerance for and dealt with varying parent and sibling moods and behaviour, maintained contacts with non-resident fathers and grandparents; and assessed and coped with teachers' bad moods. Though they did not overtly assign moral status to their actions here, their accounts show that they understood that child-adult relationships involved activity by the child as well as by the adult. Furthermore, children recounted how they negotiated pathways, in the face of the dual control and care functions of parents, making the best of control and building on the care. Looking after friends and working through with them moral issues arising from daily events and relationships was important. Indeed for many children, making and maintaining relationships with friends was one of the principal points of coming to school (cf. Alderson 2000). In addition, some children routinely did jobs around the home, without being asked to do so each time, but as delegated tasks.

Discussion

This chapter has focused on generational issues as they intersect with children's agency. I have suggested that these London children are exposed to common sets of influences on their lives, though these are cross-cut by factors such as gender and ethnicity. They also indicate through their discourse that they share understandings of their social situation – including their experience of the character of child–adult relations at home and school. The conversations I encouraged them to have with me and with each other indicate clearly their familiarity with and confirmation of each other's knowledge and experience. In Mannheim's terms, I would suggest that they have reached the second stage – they constitute 'actual generations' (see Chapter 2, page 15). I think it is questionable whether groups of children – who are positioned as subordinate to adults and thus have poor access to the means of determining their childhoods – can be said ever to form 'generational units' – the third stage Mannheim discusses (1952 [1928]: 302–12); it seems unlikely, but at both theoretical and empirical levels it is an interesting question to pursue.

Children can be seen as both reproducing and resisting the structures that shape their lives. We can see how children describe and seem to accept normative accounts of the social status of childhood, how they act within it but also in tension with it. Thus it seems that they provide clear indications that their assigned moral status does not match their moral competence as demonstrated in their daily lives. How are we to explain this discrepancy? The concept of socialisation as key to theorising childhood might be seen by mainstream sociologists as key to the problem – morally, childhood is a process of apprenticeship; individual manifestations of emergent moral behaviour do not conflict with adults' overarching understanding of the inferior moral competencies of children. The new childhood studies within sociology, with their emphasis on the child as agent, could suggest studying generational relations since that can identify how far, in specific contexts and social interactions, children have opportunities to enact moral competence.

We can start from this angle to consider how dominant adult understandings shape children's experience as a social group; how the specific siting of children's childhoods in UK social contexts allows for better understanding of their moral plight. As noted at the outset, UK children have little moral agency in the public domain, for parents are designated as responsible for their welfare and behaviour (cf. Ribbens et al. 1999). (The point is also made for US children by Cahill 1990.) Partly because of this designation and also because public space is seen as risky for children, they have very poor access on their own account to resources and facilities and therefore to decision-making. Furthermore, they have virtually no opportunities for choice at school, except at playtime. In two of the major settings of their daily lives, public spaces and school, they are assigned moral incompetence. Thus UK children, and perhaps especially city children, are largely excluded from decision-making outside the home. Indeed, the two main arenas where they are able to enact competence are in the family and in peer relationships (Hutchby and Moran-Ellis 1998a); and these arenas are obscured from public view and therefore from public understanding.

Children's varying abilities to display and develop competence according to social context is reflected in the character of their talk about family and friends as compared to talk about their experiences in public and at school. They talk about their participant activity in structuring relationships, arguing, comforting and listening. Their accounts indicate their knowledge of adults' and friends' feelings, motives and reasoning. They describe their participation in the complexities and conflicts involved in decision-making. By contrast, their talk about the formal agendas of school is commonly in terms of their lack of agency: the routinised character of the day, their status as objects of the system, teachers' authoritarian and in some cases unfair behaviour. That their views are routinely disregarded is a widespread characteristic of UK children's school experience (Alderson 2000). Indeed some children were initially non-plussed when I asked them to tell me about their school day. Since they were not actors, there was little interesting or significant for them to say. (In Chapter 6, children left school time blank and undifferentiated – see page 80).

Using children's accounts of generational issues, I aim to contribute to the development of a child standpoint: how their accounts contribute to understanding their social positioning. Their discourse on their experience and knowledge tells us that they accept childhood's inferior status to adulthood, and see both advantages and disadvantages in their social status. However, the data also reveal the uncomfortable duality of their moral status: assigned incompetence, and competence in practice. I do not know how distinctive, or how extreme the social positioning of these London children is in this respect, but I suggest that some clues may lie in the specific UK configuration of state, parent and child as to the shouldering of responsibility: the emphasis on parental (rather than societal) responsibility for children's welfare, and the complementary exclusion of children's participation in visible decision-making.

Their accounts indicate their agency in three central tasks: learning to be a good enough member of the family and culture, working on the project of their own life, and resistance to adult control. I would argue, therefore, that an important value in children's assessments of their social lives is interdependence, intertwined with the values of independence and autonomy. In making this assessment children are aligning themselves with the feminist challenge to European cultural assumptions, whereby the independent autonomous man is the measure of virtue (Grimshaw 1986). Again, it may be that the familialisation of children and of childhood in the UK somewhat accounts for children's emphasis on family relationships as the principal key to their happiness. In other societies, children's allegiances may be split more equally between family, friends, or special interests (see Chapter 10), or focused more closely on community values, or on achieving competence in economically useful skills (Chapters 3 and 7).

In this chapter I have suggested that explanations for how these London children understand childhood and assess their own daily experience can usefully be sought through study of the generational order, in social policies as they impact on children and parents, as well as in models of childhood harnessed by the adults in children's lives. Children's own agency at the intersections of these forces is shown in the broad tasks – the tasks of childhood – they undertake, and in their participation in child–adult relationships.

Note

1 'Negotiating Childhoods' (1997–9) is one of 22 research projects funded on the UK Economic and Social Research Council's Children 5–16 Programme (ref. no. L129 25 1032). I am grateful to my colleague Helen Turner, who collected data in a third primary school, and in two of the three secondary schools.

10 Childhood as a generational condition: children's daily lives in a central Finland town

Leena Alanen

Introduction

Most children of the world are born into families and spend varying proportions and lengths of their daily lives within these generationally structured 'units' in which some of the members are positioned as 'parents' while others are positioned as 'children'. This is the normal assumption of most (Western) sociology, long ago crystallized in their concepts such as the family and socialization. Mostly sociologists just assume the generational structuredness of children's lives and relationships as a (social) fact and as the basis for formulating their research questions and interpreting their results.

In this chapter, this fact will be problematized in an empirical study on the specifically *generational structuring* of children's lives. The notion of generational structuring – or 'generationing'[1] for short – refers to the complexity of social processes through which people become (are constructed as) 'children' while other people become (are constructed as) 'adults'. 'Construction' involves agency (of children and adults); it is best understood as a practical and even material process, and can be studied as a practice or a set of practices. The two generational categories of children and adults that are recurrently produced within such practices therefore stand in relations of connection and interaction, therefore interdependence: neither of them can exist without the other, what each of them is (a child, an adult) is dependent on its relation to the other, and change in one is tied to change in the other.

This profoundly relational conceptualization of children needs to be distinguished from a more common (and common-sensical) way of defining children which is based on some observable similarities or shared attributes among them, the most common one being age.[2] When children and adults are conceptualized as age groups, or cohorts, and individuals are 'classified' as children or as adults based on their age, their relations remain external and contingent, as the existence of one age group does not in any way presuppose the other.[3]

In social life, children and adults can then be connected to each other both internally and externally. The connection studied in this chapter is the former, internal one. Belonging to the category (or class) of children is something that is also the making of children themselves: childhood is socially constructed.

How this takes place, and with what effects in terms of their daily lives, now becomes a matter to explore. This is the empirical focus in the study to follow.

That processes with such generationing effects do exist in the social world is to make, at this point, merely a theoretical assumption, for social processes are never directly visible; it is only through their effects that they may become identified. There seem to be, however, effects that are impressive enough to warrant such an assumption (e.g. Mayall 1994b; Qvortrup 1994), and to start theorizing *generation* as a 'structuring structure' (Bourdieu 1990), analogical to the structure of gender as theorized in feminist studies, or the proto-sociological structure of class. For both everyday knowledge and the evidence accumulated in social scientific studies on childhood demonstrate that being a child (or an adult) does make a difference (or differences) in terms of one's activities, opportunities, experiences and identities, as well as the relationships between members of the two categories.

Two further rationales can be given for such a *relational*[4] approach to childhood and generation. First, one of the grounding axioms of Childhood Studies has been that childhood is to be understood as a social and historical construction and therefore the nature (or 'essence') of childhood will not be given by any set of past or present observations and experiences of actual living children and their lives. To understand childhood would require the understanding of the whole set of material, social and discursive processes, in interplay, through which childhood is daily (re-)produced as a social, and specifically generational, condition.

Secondly, not everything observable in the lives of the little beings that in everyday parlance we call children can be assumed to follow from their being children, whatever the local and historical construction of childness is. For children are not only children: they are also boys and girls, so that their childhoods are also gender ordered. A similar case can be argued for class, 'race' and ethnicity: also these are structures that 'determine' the lives, experiences and understandings of the children we know and study. But while gender, class, 'race' or ethnicity, their constructed nature, and the material, social and discursive processes of their construction have all been abundantly explored, analyzed and theorized by social scientists, *generation*[5] (or the generational order, comparable to class structure or gender order) has been slow to catch attention, even among those who work within Childhood Studies. One of the aims of this chapter is therefore to develop the notions of generation and generational order.

Like class and gender, generation cannot be assumed to operate on restricted domains of social life; besides families, so too schools, day-care centres and other institutionalized domains for children are further obvious sites for generationing. And like gendering and 'classing', perhaps even 'racing', generationing can be assumed to take place also outside such child-marked institutions, in fact in every domain of social life – in working life and in politics just as much as in the cultural field – and quite irrespective of whether concrete children are actually 'seen' to be present and acting in them. In the empirical study considered below, some of these generationing processes are traced across several arenas in which children daily live their lives.

A specific interest in exploring the generational structures within which childhood as a social position is daily produced and lived concerns children's agency. In a relational framework, agency clearly will not be restricted to the micro-constructionist understanding of being a social actor. Rather, it now refers to the 'powers' (or lack of them) of those positioned as a child to influence, organize, coordinate and control events taking place in their everyday worlds. Such powers are best understood as possibilities (and limitations) of action and as determined by the structures within which people are positioned as children. Therefore, in order to detect the range and nature of the agency of concrete, living children, the exploration needs to be oriented towards identifying the generational structures from which children's powers (or lack of them) derive: the source of their agency in their capacity of children is to be found in the social organization of generational relations.

In summary, a relational methodology such as I have started to sketch above, will need to begin from children's lived and experienced childhoods – their daily lives as enacted and experienced by them. It is then a clear case of a standpoint methodology.[6]

The study: data and analysis

The data for the study were collected with twenty 9–10 year old children living in a typical suburb of a middle-sized Finnish town. The children and their parents were first contacted in spring 1998 when they all were in the third grade of the suburban primary school in the same class. The main part of the data was collected through interviews, first in pairs and later individually. Before the interviews, I spent a lot of time in school, being present in the classroom, getting to know the children, going out with them during breaks, walking on the yard with them, talking and playing with them (after being invited to do so), having lunch together with them at school, and walking home with them after school. Pair interviews were conducted in their school during school time, and for these sessions, children chose a friend from the class with whom she or he wanted to be interviewed. All the children in the class volunteered eagerly for these discussions.

Later in the year data collection continued by individual interviews with eight of the original twenty children, the sessions being combined with walks home from school or they took place in the evening at the child's home. Interviewing was then often combined with talk with parents and siblings.

Analysis of the data was started by constructing 'inventories' of the daily life for each of the participating children. These inventories were then compared with each other to find similarities and differences in ways in which children through their everyday activities seem to relate to people, activities and things. Based on comparisons between the inventories, a number of domains of daily life were identified which were typical in the studied group of children and also relatively separate from each other, also in the subjective sense of the children themselves: they were part of their everyday knowledge and discourse.

Childhood domains: identification and analysis

Children in the Western world mostly start their 'career' as children by being born into a family and becoming members of such a unit; they depend significantly on it for the material, social and cultural resources that they deploy in the making of their particular childhoods. The degree of this formative dependency on a family of one's own does, of course, vary transnationally but even among children living in the same country, region or locality, such as the home suburb of the children studied here. Most of the twenty children have lived in the same suburb since they were born, perhaps having only moved house within the area. But there are also other features of life history which the children share: all of them have been in day-care outside home before starting school, many of them all through their pre-school years – a direct consequence of the fact that most of their parents, like most Finnish parents in general, work full-time outside home.

But such shared experiences of extra-familial worlds notwithstanding, family – or home at least – continues to be a significant site for children's daily activities. In addition, other sites, or *domains* of everyday life, were identified by reading analytically children's descriptions of

1   their daily activities, hobbies and pursuits, and use of time in them, the initiation, planning and coordination of daily activities;
2   the web of people with whom children do things together, such as parents (both own and other children's parents), siblings, friends and mates, other kids in the neighbourhood, teachers, club members and leaders, coaches, members and directors of choir or orchestra, people they meet at the college for music, at dance school or riding school, and other daily activities; and
3   their understandings of what these activities are pursued for, where the personal significance of each of the activities lies for them, why they participate in them on a regular basis, what else they would like to do and why.

Four such domains were identified from these accounts, and named commonsensically as 'Family', 'School', 'Friendships' and 'Personal Interests'.

All the children participating in the study moved (almost) daily within all of these domains; they were to a greater or lesser extent part of every child's life. However, some children moved more on one domain than another, and related to the other three domains in a patterned way. These patterns, and the domains themselves, are described below as the domains of children who appeared to be 'strong' (or 'empowered') in the particular domain, in terms of having access to and knowing how to use the material, social and/or cultural resources relevant for the domain specific activities. There is, of course, variation among the children 'strong' in each domain; the descriptions here attempt to catch their typicalities.

Family

Inka is one of altogether seven children (out of twenty), whose daily life takes place predominantly within the *Family* domain: her daily activities outside school take place mainly indoors, either at her own home or at the home of a 'best friend' living downstairs in the same block of apartments. She also spends many weekends with her mother at their summer cottage, near grandmother's house, and her mother (a lone parent) also takes her every week to enjoy an hour of riding, or swimming at the city swimming hall. Often a friend of Inka's is invited to come along too. Inka enjoys doing housework and making things pretty and tidy in their household; there is not much to do as her mother takes care of most things, including shopping and cooking; however, Inka is expected to manage her own room. The weekly rotation of activities and going to places is largely managed by the parents in agreement: Inka lives in a bi-nuclear family situation and spends every second weekend, and some holiday time, at her father's new family. There too, with her two 'social siblings', her life is filled with activities and relationships of the familial kind: TV-watching and playing games together, going to the sauna, shopping and going on outings with the new family.

Friendships

Inka, of course, has friends and they are important to her, but in contrast to her fairly small circle of play mates, the number of friends Maija is able to list, and the frequency with which she sees them is far beyond Inka's circle of friends as is her idea of what friendships are for. Maija meets her friends – or friends of her friends, for there is a continual process of weaving of new children into the network – mostly out-of-doors, as she moves with other children in the yards between the blocks or the little parks and woods, of which there are many in the suburb. They are often in large groups, and Maija is particularly interested (as well as good at) getting to know new characters, preferably older than she is. *Friendships*, Maija herself pointed out, are the most important thing in her life: without friends her daily life would be grey and dull. In the world of friendships, she asserts, she is learning all kinds of new things and competencies all the time, and the experience of becoming and being competent is paramount to her and best secured for her within this domain – not, for instance, in the School domain.

School

School names here an activity domain which does not refer simply to school as the obligatory place for children to go for purposes of learning. For Sami, the concrete school where he goes, with its schedules of learning, is at times a dull place and some days really boring, but then some school subjects and events can be very interesting, too. The (rare) moments of fascination in school are of the kind as when 'one learns to use the pencil [in art classes] in a different way, so as to produce a thick or a thin stroke' (Sami). Perpetually learning new things, getting to know how to do things by oneself, the experience that one grows in knowledge – all of this is significant for him, and they are also the kinds of experiences he is perpetually hunting for outside school. Sami is on the lookout for such possibilities by joining the school choir, the scouts and even the cooking club that meets once a week in the school. He goes often to the local library and reads a lot, he also eagerly tries new programs on his parents' computer at home, and contemplates starting to play some instrument, for he's dreaming of joining the school brass band. Having a lot of friends is not something to look forward to in itself; much more important is what kind of people they are and what you can do with them. It therefore also does not matter if they are girls or babies or adults, and in fact Sami confesses (lowering his voice) that he enjoys being with both babies and girls, and he particularly likes to be around and participate in discussions when colleagues and friends of his parents are visiting his home. Being alone is also no problem, and he often keeps himself to himself, likes to be quiet without therefore feeling lonely.

Personal interests

For Pauliina, having to go to school, and everything that this implies, is the least interesting thing in her life. It is of course essential to cope with the demands of school, but 'real' life waits elsewhere, and this is where she can freely follow her personal interests. In her case at the moment, they are musical: she travels every week to the college of music downtown, for lessons in playing as well as in theory of music, and she also practises playing at home. She also recently looked up details of the entrance examination of the city children's choir, went and passed the test and now travels by bus to choir rehearsals once or twice a week. The exact number of friends is hard for her to specify, for friends are those who currently share her interests, with whom she can talk about her interests and who enjoy doing the same kind of things, even though she may see them just once or twice a week. Pilvi is another child whose daily life is significantly dominated by activities in the *Personal Interests* domain. Differently from Pauliina, her personal interests are in sports, but as for Pauliina, for her, too, the experience of feeling successful in her favourite activity and being among people who share her personal interest is the driving motive for continuing, even competitively, her (burgeoning) career in sports.

When asked, all the children talk easily about their families, friends, school and what they like to do in their free time; also their accounts of daily activities show that they all move in and about all of the four domains distinguished here and exemplified by individual cases of children. Although no domain is completely cut from each other, for any one child, there are clear indications of an order existing between the domains in (nearly) each case. As for the few children presented above, so the rest of the children can be categorized according to the main activity domain in their lives; we therefore have a relatively large group of 'Family (domain)' children, and smaller groups of 'Friendships' children, 'School' children and finally 'Personal Interests' children:[7]

'Family' children: Anni, Ari, Elina, Esa, Inka, Oona, Otto   (4 girls, 3 boys)
'Friendships' children: Maija, Meri, Minna   (3 girls)
'School' children: Sami, Satu   (1 girl, 1 boy)
'Personal Interests' children: Pauliina, Pilvi   (2 girls)

Based on the identification of the domains, a relational analysis of each of them followed, with the aim of exploring the existing *generational positions* for children to take and enact, within each of them.[8]

Indicators for the positioning of the ('empirical') children as expressly 'children' within the domain in question – that is within its particular generational structure – consist of the various home *rules* by which children's actions in the domain are organized, coordinated and controlled, as well as the *responsibilities* which they assume (or are made to assume) within domains. The justifications given to the rules and responsibilities and known to them, whether they accepted and followed them or not, contribute to the 'input' side of children's positioning within the domains. The reverse, or 'outcome' side of children's positioning is looked at from the standpoint of *dependence* and *independence* as experienced and practised by the children. The degree of (in)dependency in occupying a position within a generational structure, and in maintaining (or expanding) a specific structural practice, is indicated by children's experiences and feelings about self-care and of times being away from home or from family, of feelings raised by times spent alone, and of experiences of having a say in matters important to and affecting oneself.

'Childing' practices

From domains and positions the analytical strategy was to proceed towards identifying the social *practices* within which children in their everyday lives relate to objects in their environment (both people and 'things') in relatively enduring ways, and to identify children's own contributions to maintaining or changing their generational position within the domain. Thus some of these patterns appeared as the everyday practices of *generationing*, that is, as the practices through which one first becomes, or is made, a 'child', in relation to non-children. This 'becoming' is by no means a natural or automatic process: it involves active construction, therefore agency, at every step.

The evidence of some children being both objectively and subjectively 'strong' in one domain, others in the other domains, gives sufficient reason to ask: what separates the domains from each other in the sense of constituting them as different kinds of power bases[9] for children? Possible answers to such questions are sought in the data first by looking at differences in the rules and responsibilities that children identify as regulators of their daily activities. There were rules that in fact all the children could recount, the most notable one being about coming on schooldays straight home, first sitting down to do homework (Friday being the exception), and having a snack before watching TV, or going out, or playing with friends.

From the data it appears that the 'Family' children were able to list many more as well as more exact rules and responsibilities compared to the other children:

'Family' children

- time schedules: mealtime, coming in from outdoors, bedtimes (at 21 hrs)
- call the parent(s) when at home from school
- not allowed to watch 'certain kinds' of movies or TV programmes
- friends who may come to child's home while parents are away, and number of them at a time
- not to use bad language
- to obey parents
- not to mess up places when at home after school
- to help in housework by keeping own room tidy
- not to use cutting knives, electric stove or other electric appliances when alone at home

The lack of clear rules in the case of children of the other domains does not mean that they would be allowed to behave as they pleased. Most of the children confirmed that they currently have no such rules to obey, but that in many cases they nevertheless tended to act in similar ways. The same went for responsibilities: they would 'help with the housework anyway', even liked to do specific tasks such as baking or cooking a meal for the family; they also 'often called their parents after school and had a chat over the phone' or left a note on the table to tell homecoming parents where they were and when they would be coming back.

Such 'habits' of children, in the absence of clearly stated rules and responsibilities, inform about the degree of self-care practised by children. Even further indications of self-care by non-'Family' children were found:

'Friendships' children

- travel downtown (e.g. to swimming hall) with friends
- make snacks for oneself during daytime, also evening
- arrange often to stay overnight at friends' homes

'School' children

- wake up on school mornings by oneself (alarm clock)
- take care of leaving in time for school
- travel by bus downtown alone
- spend a lot of time alone, doing one's own things

'Personal Interests' children

- wake up in the mornings by oneself (alarm clock)
- take care of leaving in time for school
- travel by bus downtown alone
- take care of matters related to personal interests (music lessons, training sessions, choir rehearsals)
- do homework from school autonomously (also on Fridays to have the weekend free for personal interests)

Based on this evidence from the data, there seem to be some clear differences between the domains in the extent of routinely practised self-care and also the confidence with which children say they take care of their everyday matters: the 'Family' children display least self-care while the 'Personal Interests' children display more than the other groups, the two other groups being somewhere in-between.

The differences found to exist between the domains allow the first conclusion to be made: *being a child* clearly means different things for children strong in different domains. The routines of everyday life as given by the kinds and numbers of familial rules and responsibilities as well as the extent of children's self-care practices highlight the material and social aspects of 'childness' (Wartofsky 1983; Cook-Gumperz 1991). The pattern of differences shown above is confirmed also by children's self-positioning of themselves as 'children' (or alternatively something else) and generally their own discourse on childhood: only the 'Family' children would present extensive lists of the advantages of their (still) being a child, as well as disadvantages connected to the position of the child. And each of them confirmed that at present they preferred being a child. Children of the other three domains were very much more vague about such topics. Either they wished to detach themselves from the category of 'children' by using finer distinctions than just child vs. adult, as when defining themselves as young persons (in the case of 'Friendships' children), or they were plainly uninterested in having conversations on the topic at all, and found it difficult or irrelevant to position themselves on some generational scale ('School' and 'Personal Interests' children). 'School' children preferred instead to give long narratives about the many skills and competencies they already have, emphasizing the personal significance of continuously learning to do and understand new things, and linking this to their own growing (but not to growing up!). This simply made irrelevant for them a hierarchy such as the child vs. adult. In the case of the 'Personal Interests' children, childness was mentioned merely as a common – and annoying – attribution to small-sized people, as Pilvi felt she was herself, with her less than 140 cm, which she felt prevented her from progress in her gymnastics career as quickly as she would like. For Pauliina – the other 'Personal Interests' child – being a child meant the equally annoying situation that one had to live in a family, which brought about a number of limitations to her personal projects. But 'there are not many alternatives, are there, as somebody has to provide you with food and housing and clothes and that kinds of things, so you just have to tolerate the situation . . .' (Pauliina).

A second conclusion to be drawn from this part of analysis is that there exist a number of different generationing practices in which also children actively participate, and are in fact constrained to participate in through their necessary dependence on adult-led households. One of the generating practices found in the study seems to be, more solidly than the others, a 'childing practice', in that children's participation in this practice tended to (re)produce a distinct 'child' position for children to occupy, with rules and responsibilities prescribing the position and bringing for the children following the prescription, as well as subjectively experienced advantages and disadvantages, a self-identification and a (mainly positive) self-image of childness. This is the practice that is most clearly dependent, firstly, on the quasi-autonomous family household as its *material* basis, secondly, on close connections between members of the family, also the larger family of grandparents, cousins, aunts, uncles and godparents as its *social* basis and, thirdly, a particular discourse of 'the (nuclear) family' as its *cultural* (semiotic) basis.

The other generationing practices have their material, social and cultural bases mainly elsewhere, partly, it seems, in other non-familial institutions (educational institutions) and organizations (sports organizations, youth organizations, public/welfare state services, such as libraries or children's clubs). The social relationships which incorporate children to these non-familial practices, and their semiosis (meaning-making), bring within the reach of children a variety of resources, and therefore opportunities for negotiating their own position, also in relation to their family lives. The always provisional result of such negotiations is an unstable position, therefore one too that the children in the study were unwilling to describe in terms of any popular discourse of childhood, as they were known to them. Interpreted within a developmental discourse, the childhoods of the non-'Family' children certainly would soon begin to look risky and dangerous, and more supervision, guidance and control (by adults) would be recommended to protect the children from the looming dangers. The interpretation that presents itself when the very same childhoods are approached from children's standpoint is very different, and the risks and dangers that children may well meet are to be looked for elsewhere: in changes of societal distributions of material, social and cultural resources and children's possibilities to access them alone, with other children or with sympathetic and supportive adults. In times of recession, with high rates of unemployment among parents of the children living in the suburb studied here, and the simultaneous dismantling of welfare state provisions and public services, the programmatics of child-friendly politics is clear enough.

The next question asked was: why do the practices of childhood differ in the four domains, what are the structuring 'mechanisms' responsible for producing each practice? This was done by asking 'retroductive' questions about what makes the different practices possible: which kinds of resources (or 'capitals', cf. Bourdieu 1990), or 'powers', need to be available for the person (agent) to reproduce the practice in question, and even to strengthen and elaborate his or her position within it, and in which ways is access to such resources provided or not, in the normal course of children's daily (or weekly) life. Other structures and mechanisms may also help to sustain the position-holding and the practice, whereas the absence of some resources may predispose children to one practice rather than another.

Generational structures

Why is the generationing practice a familial, 'childing' practice in the case of some children, while in the case of others it may be of the 'Friendships' type, the 'School' type, or the 'Personal Interests' type? Mainstream sociology would probably suggest as explanatory 'variables', for instance the beliefs that parents have about children, their ideas about the family, their education or socio-economic status, size of family, gender. A relational analysis would need to explore the contextual resources to which children have, or have not, access and which therefore, either directly or indirectly, link children to other social structures further away from their everyday domains. The material organization of childhood, in Western societies, is basically through children's household membership, and while some resources needed for the construction of childhoods exist in the household, the household also to a great extent mediates children's access to material, social and cultural resources outside the family/household. Other mediators exist, too. Above, the provision made by public services, institutions and organizations was mentioned. The suburb – as the physical and social environment of children's daily life – in itself provides resources: space and things (playgrounds, woods and forests, parks, clubhouses, school buildings and school yards, library, the mall, sporting grounds, ice rinks, . . .) and, of course, people in all of these places.

The number of resources that make possible particular generationing practices (such as the ones identified above), is potentially huge and their coming together a complex process of interplay, in which the children's active negotiations are also a constitutive factor. To account for a total 'generational structure' consisting of all existing childhood practices would require the investigation of a large number of such linking processes. In the case of the children studied here, they span over their own life-time, and even longer, as some of the structural elements (such as the planning and building of suburbs) were already constructed before they arrived there, sometimes by 'people long dead' (Archer 1995).

Although the generational structures involved in producing the four generationing practices can only crudely be sketched, in a small-scale study like this,
the information below indicates that there are real differences also between the
structures: the 'Family' children seem to have lived in circumstances of more
limited access to resources, and the resources are predominantly provided by
the neighbourhood, the child's own family as well as the larger family, whereas
the 'Friendships' children and the 'School' children seem to have had access to
'social capital' (cf. Bourdieu 1990) through relationships with other people
(children and adults) and through experiences of other places (they have lived
also outside the suburb or do a lot of travelling):

'Family' children

- have lived all their lives in suburb
- half of them are only children
- live in blocks of flats (both low rise and high rise)
- before starting school: a mixture of home care and day-care
- summer cottage (in a few cases)
- family travels to visit larger family

'Friendships' children

- have lived all their lives in suburb
- largest families/several siblings
- bi-nuclear or reconstituted families (social siblings)
- live in blocks of flats or one-family house
- summers spent at summer cottage (with cousins) or at home

'School' children

- have moved to suburb from other town
- smallest families
- live in terraced house
- summer trips abroad with family
- a lot of family travelling (also alone)
- parents are professionals

'Personal Interests' children

- have lived all their lives in suburb
- live in terraced house and (low rise) blocks of flats
- nuclear families

Trajectories

Based on such an analysis of domain-specific resources of power, some of the
social trajectories of childhood can be sketched, in terms of the transitions chil-

dren have already made, or are in the process of making, from the domain and its typical practices to a new one, but of course two or even three practices can also be maintained simultaneously. Such trajectories suggest some of the possible routes that children have travelled within the overall generational order. Observing such trajectories helps furthermore to focus the analysis also towards asking further questions about the resources necessary for generationing practices to be sustained, as well as about the mechanisms of moving children from one practice to another, thereby transforming their own 'childness'.

It would be far too deterministic to assume that children are born to, and stay within the confines of just one dominant domain – in which they are presently 'strong' – one generationing practice and one (although very complex) generational structure. Children can and do display strength and powers in more than one domain. And as the scheme below shows, many of the children are beginning to move to a new domain and even two domains.

From 'Family'

to	–	Anni
to	'Friendships'	Inka, Oona, Jussi
to	'Friendships' to 'Personal Interests'	Otto
to	'Personal Interests'	Elina
to	'Personal Interests' to 'School'	Esa

From 'Friendships'

to	'Personal Interests'	Maija, Meri
to	–	Minna

From 'School'

to	'Personal Interests'	Satu, Sami

From 'Personal Interests'

to	'Friendships'	Pauliina, Pilvi

A summarizing conclusion from the patterns in these movements presented in the above scheme would be in terms of the generational structures which 'determine' the four activity domains on the left side of the scheme: the question then is, what is it in the structures, in their combining of material, social and cultural resources that make possible, if not constrain, a movement to another domain. The data suggest that the strengths, or the powers, which children gain by participating in the 'childing' mode of generationing, are conducive to their movement both to a 'Friendships' mode and a 'Personal Interests' mode, while the 'School' domain seems to provide resources for acquiring 'Personal Interests'. However the number of the children in this study is small and the nature of data such as to merely raise the question – now, however, on the structural level, and not on the level of individual capacities and their development.

Conclusion

The theme running through this chapter is 'generation'. Empirically, the chapter has explored the daily lives and relationships of a group of 9–10 year old children living in a particular (Nordic, Finnish, small town suburban) context, with the aim of finding out, what it is in that context that tends to give those social relationships a specifically *generational* shape, thus making them into particular kinds of childhoods and identifying the 'little beings' studied here as expressly 'children'. Methodologically, this approach assumes *relational* thinking, this in turn being based on a view (an ontology) of the social world as consisting basically of relations, and relations between relations (or structures).

The childhoods and the differences among them that were detected in the empirical study now also become explicable, but this time not in terms of the social, class, ethnic and so on background, culture or the local circumstances of the children in the study (as conventionally done in analyses with 'substantialist' focus), but by detecting the both direct and indirect, invisible relations through which children are firmly embedded in structured sets of relations larger than their very immediate local relations and potentially extending as far as the global social system. In a small-scale study, such as the one presented here, a beginning can be made to show the containment of children's childhoods within larger structures, on the condition that a relational notion of the socially constructed essence of (any) childhood is accepted as a methodological starting point.

This opens a final stage in the logic of this study in which we can begin to collect pieces for an explanation for the daily lives of the children participating in the study. If the possibility of practising a particular childhood will depend on the availability of and access to specific material, social and cultural (semiotic) resources, then it is relevant to ask how the resources necessary for the practice in question are socially distributed and made available (or not) for children in general to deploy. Resource distributions are socially constructed facts within a historically existing society, and so are the mechanisms of distribution, of which there are many: through markets or through families, directly targeted on children, built into public services and made accessible on an equal basis, or made dependent on purchasing, or readily available in the everyday material and social environment. Finland is a wealthy Nordic country, but with a history not far away from rural traditions of poverty and hard work; it still retains a fairly well-developed welfare state and has the smallest differentials of wealth and income in the West. The resources and their distribution that become available for the suburban children studied here may therefore well differ from that available to children in other times and countries, as also shown in the chapters of this book. Links between the different childhoods exist, however, although a small-scale study such as presented in this chapter can merely point to the large-scale contextual enablements and constraints on the regional, national and even transnational level that exist also for the childhoods studied here. More data and also data of other kinds – historical and statistical – are needed in order to link these suburban childhoods to such global structures and mechanisms, of which they – and other childhoods – too are part.

Acknowledgement

The empirical study discussed here – 'Negotiating Childhoods: Children in the Generational Order' – was funded by the Academy of Finland (ref. no. S8460).

Notes

1 In making the noun into a verb a parallel conceptual move is made as the feminist move from 'gender' to 'gendering'. Cf. also Morgan (1999: 16) who argues that also 'family' is best seen as 'less of a noun and more of an adjective or, possibly, a verb'. In a similar way, in this chapter it is suggested that it is helpful to see also 'child' as a verb, and possibly also as an adjective expressing the social quality of childness.
2 Attribution of age, however, is probably one of the central (cultural) mechanisms in the generationing practices of modern Western societies.
3 See Sayer (1992: 88–92) on the logic of internal, or necessary relations, and of external, contingent relations.
4 On relational methodologies in sociology, see e.g. Bhaskar (1979), Bourdieu (1990: 123–39, 1998: 1–13); Bourdieu and Wacquant (1992: 94–8), Swartz (1997: 6), Manicas (1998) and Scott (1998). Pierre Bourdieu argues strongly for relationalism and contrasts it with a mode of thought he (following Cassirer) calls 'substantialism' which 'leads people to recognize no realities except those that are available to direct intuition in ordinary experience, individuals and groups'. Relationalism (or relationism; Scott 1998), identifies the real not with substances but with relations, and sociology, according to this view, is the analysis of these relations, that is: 'relative positions and relations between positions' (Bourdieu 1990: 126, 1998: 3).
5 For theorizing class as internal relations see e.g. Wright (1985, 1989), and gender e.g. Connell 1987.
6 For standpoint methodology in sociology, see e.g. Smith (1988: 105–47) on women's standpoint; Alanen (1990, 1992) on children's standpoint. Cf. feminist 'standpoint epistemologies' (e.g. Alcoff and Potter 1993; Henwood et al. 1998).
7 In this list, fourteen of the original twenty children are included. Two of the remaining six are hard to categorize because of the scant information they chose to share with me during the pair interview (they were interviewed together). Four other children were also not listed, as they proved not to be 'strong' in any of the four domains. Their cases will be analyzed elsewhere.
8 It needs to be assumed that the domains are structured also in other ways: gendered, classed . . . In this analysis, the focus is solely on their generational structuredness. Within the scope of the space given here, only the generational positions within the 'Family' domain – the most clearly childing domain – can be presented; the other three domains are merely compared to the 'Family' domain.
9 Cf. Bourdieu's notion of fields (e.g. Bourdieu and Wacquant 1992: 94–115), and of power as resources or 'capitals', each form of them specific to field (ibid., 115–20; Swartz 1997: 65–94).

Bibliography

Alanen, L. (1990) 'Rethinking socialization, the family and childhood', *Sociological Studies of Child Development*, 3: 13–28.

Alanen, L. (1992) *Modern Childhood? Exploring the 'Child Question' in Sociology*, Research Report 50, Jyväskylä: University of Jyväskylä.

Alanen, L. and Bardy, M. (1990) *Childhood as a Social Phenomenon: National Report Finland*, Eurosocial Report 36/7, Vienna: European Centre.

Alcoff, L. and Potter, E. (eds) (1993) *Feminist Epistemologies*, New York and London: Routledge.

Alderson, P. (1993) *Children's Consent to Surgery*, Buckingham: Open University Press.

Alderson, P. (2000) 'School students' views on school councils and daily life at school', *Children and Society*, 14, 2: 121–34.

Almond, D. (1999) 'Leave time for imaginations', London: The Independent Newspaper – 15th July 1999.

Archer, M. (1995) *Realist Social Theory: The Morphogenetic Approach*, Cambridge: Cambridge University Press.

Aries, P. (1972) *Centuries of Childhood*, Harmondsworth: Penguin.

Asian Development Bank (1995) *Escaping the Poverty Trap, Lessons from Asia*, ADB Report No. 010394, Tokyo: Asian Development Bank.

Attias-Donfut, C. (1988) *Sociologie des Générations: L'Empreinte du Temps*, Paris: Presses Universitaires de France.

BBWFT (Bundesministerium für Bildung, Wissenschaft, Forschung und Technologie) (1996) *Grund und Strukturdaten*, Bonn.

Becker, H.A. (ed.) (1992) *Dynamics of Cohort and Generations Research*, Amsterdam: Thesis Publishers.

Becker, H.A. and Hermkens, P.L.J. (eds) (1993) *Solidarity of Generations: Demographic, Economic and Social Change, and its Consequences*, Vols I-II. Amsterdam: Thesis Publishers.

Becker, R. (1997) Generationen und sozialer Wandel – eine Einleitung, in R. Becker (ed.) *Generationen und Sozialer Wandel*, Opladen: Leske und Budrich.

Belle, D. (ed.) (1989) *Children's Social Networks and Social Supports*, New York: Wiley.

Beresford, B. (1997) *Personal Accounts: Involving Disabled Children in Research*, Norwich: Social Policy Research Unit.

Bernstein, B. (1971) 'On the classification and framing of educational knowledge', in M. Young (ed.) *Knowledge and Control*, London: Collier-Macmillan.

BFSFJ (Bundesminister für Familie, Senioren, Frauen und Jugend) (1997) *Die Familie im Spiegel der amtlichen Statistik*, Bonn.

Bhaskar, R. (1979) *The Possibility of Naturalism*, Hemel Hempstead: Harvester Wheatsheaf.

Bird, C. (ed.) (1998) *The Stolen Children: Their Stories*, Sydney: Random House.

Björnberg, U. (1996) 'Children's rights in a dual-earner family context in Sweden', in H. Wintersberger (ed.) *Children on the Way from Marginality to Citizenship, Childhood Policies: Conceptual and Practical Issues*, Eurosocial Report 61, Vienna: European Centre.

Blatchford, P. (1998) *Social Life in School*, London: Falmer Press.

Bornstein, M. (ed.) (1991) *Cultural Approaches to Parenting*, London: Lawrence Erlbaum.

Bourdieu, P. (1971) 'Systems of education and systems of thought', in M. Young (ed.) *Knowledge and Control*, London: Collier-Macmillan.

Bourdieu, P. (1990) *In Other Words*, Cambridge: Polity Press.

Bourdieu, P. (1998) *Practical Reason*, Stanford: Stanford University Press.

Bourdieu, P. and Wacquant, L.J.D. (1992) *An Invitation to Reflexive Sociology*, Cambridge: Polity Press.

Boyden, J. (1990) 'A comparative perspective on the globalization of childhood', in A. James and A. Prout (eds) *Constructing and Reconstructing Childhood: Contemporary Issues in the Sociological Study of Childhood*, Basingstoke: Falmer Press.

Boyden, J. (1997) 'Childhood and the policy makers', in A. James and A. Prout (eds) *Constructing and Reconstructing Childhood: Contemporary Issues in the Sociological Study of Childhood*, Second edition, London: Falmer Press.

Boyden, J., Ling, B. and Myers, W. (1998) *What Works for Working Children*, Stockholm: Rädda Barnen and UNICEF.

Bradley, H. (1996) *Fractured Identities: Changing Patterns of Inequality*, Cambridge: Polity Press.

Brannen, J. (1995) 'Young people and their contribution to household work', *Sociology*, 29: 317–38.

Brannen, J., Dodd, K., Oakley, A. and Storey, P. (1994) *Young People, Health and Family Life*, Buckingham: Open University Press.

Briggs, J. (1970) *Never in Anger*, Cambridge, Mass.: Harvard University Press.

Burman, E. (1994) *Deconstructing Developmental Psychology*, London: Routledge.

Butler, I. and Williamson, H. (1994) *Children Speak. Children, Trauma and Social Work*, Essex: Longman.

Cahill, S.E. (1990) 'Childhood in public life: reaffirming biographic divisions', *Social Problems*, 37, 3: 390–402.

Carvel, J. (1999) 'A vision under the microscope', London: The Guardian Newspaper – 2nd November 1999.

Cashmore, J., Dolby, R. and Brennan, D. (1995) *Systems Abuse*, Sydney: New South Wales Child Protection Council.

Cassirer, E. (1969) *The Philosophy of Enlightenment*, Princeton, N.J.: Princeton University Press.

Chang, C. and Koster, K. (1994) *Pastoralists at the Periphery*, Tucson: University of Arizona Press.

Cheal, D. (1989) 'Strategies of resource management in household economics: Moral economy or political economy?', in R. Wilk (ed.) *The Household Economy: Reconsidering the Domestic Mode of Production*, London: Westview Press.

Chisholm, R. (1979) 'When should the state take over?', *Legal Service Bulletin* 4: 133–8.

Christensen, P. and James, A. (2000) 'Childhood diversity and commonality: Some methodological insights', in P. Christensen and A. James (eds) *Research with Children: Perspectives and Practices*, London: Falmer Press.

Christensen, P., James, A. and Jenks, C. (2000) 'All we needed to do was blow the whistle: Children's embodiment of time', in S. Cunningham Burley (ed.) *Exploring the Body*, London: Macmillan.

Cleaves, F.W. (1982) *The Secret History of the Mongols*, Cambridge, Mass.: Harvard University Press.

Cloke, C. and Davies, M. (eds) (1995) *Participation and Empowerment in Child Protection*, London: John Wiley & Sons.

Connell, R.W. (1987) *Gender and Power*, Cambridge: Polity Press.

Conner, C. (1998) 'Primary changes' in C. Richards and P. H. Taylor (eds) *How Shall we School Our Children?*, London: Falmer.

Cook-Gumperz, J. (1991) 'Children's construction of Achildness', in B. Scales, M. Almy, A. Nicolopoulou and S. Ervin-Tripp (eds) *Play and the Social Context of Development in Early Care and Education*, New York: Teachers College Press.

Corker, M. and French, S. (1999) *Disability Discourse,* Buckingham: Open University Press.

Corrigan, P. (1979) *Schooling the Smash Street Kids*, London: Macmillan.

Corsten, M. (1999) 'The Time of generations', *Time & Society*, 8, 2: 249–72.

Crompton, R. (1998) *Class and Stratification*, Cambridge: Polity Press.

Cullingford, C. (1997) 'Parents from the point of view from their children', *Education Review*, 49, 1: 47–56.

Davies, B. (1982) *Life in the Classroom and Playground*, London: Routledge and Kegan Paul.

Diezinger, A. and Rerrich, M.S. (1998) 'Die Modernisierung der Fürsorglichkeit in der alltäglichen Lebensführung junger Frauen: Neuerfindung des Albekannten?', in M. Oechsle and B. Geissler (eds) *Die ungleiche Gleichheit*, Opladen: Leske und Budrich.

du Bois-Reymond, M. (2000) 'Negotiating families', in M. du Bois-Reymond, H. Sünker and H. Krüger (eds) *Childhood in Europe. Approaches – Trends – Findings*, New York: Peter Lang.

Dubet, F. (1991) *Les Lycéens,* Paris: Seuil.

Dubet, F. (1994) *Sociologie de l'Expérience*, Paris: Seuil.

Dunn, J. (1988) *The Beginnings of Social Understanding*, Oxford: Basil Blackwell.

Dunn, J. (1996) 'Family conversations and the development of social understanding', in B. Bernstein and J. Brannen (eds) *Children, Research and Policy*, London: Taylor and Francis.

Ecarius, J. (1998) 'Generation – ein Grindbegriff', in J. Ecarius (ed.) *Was will die jüngere mit der älteren Generation?* Opladen: Leske und Budrich.

Ennew, J. (1994) 'Time for children or time for adults', in J. Qvortrup, M. Bardy, G. Sgritta and H. Wintersberger (eds) *Childhood Matters: Social Theory, Practice and Politics*, Aldershot: Avebury.

Finch, J. (1986) 'Age', in R. Burgess (ed.) *Key Variables in Social Investigation*, London: Routledge and Kegan Paul.

Finch, J. (1989) *Family Obligations and Social Change*, Cambridge: Polity Press.

Finch, J. and Mason, J. (1993) *Negotiating Family Responsibilities*, London: Routledge.

Friedman, K. (1984) 'Households as income-pooling units', in J. Smith, I. Wallerstein and H.-D. Evans (eds) *Households and the World Economy*, Beverly Hills: Sage.

Funder, K. (ed.) (1996) *Citizen Child: Australian Law and Children's Rights*, Melbourne: Australian Institute of Family Matters.

Geissler, B. and Öchsle, M. (1996) *Lebensplanung junger Frauen. Zur widersprüchlichen Modernisierung weiblicher Lebensläufe,* Weinheim: Deutscher Studien Verlag.

Giddens, A. (1979) *Central Problems in Social Theory: Action, Structure and Contradiction in Social Analysis*, London: Macmillan Education Ltd.

Giddens, A. (1981) 'Agency, institution, and time-space analysis', in K. Knorr-Cetina and A.V. Cicourel (eds) *Advances in Social Theory and Methodology*, London: Routledge and Kegan Paul.

Giddens, A. (1984) *The Constitution of Society*, Oxford: Polity Press.

Goddard, C. and Carew, R. (1993) *Responding to Children*, Melbourne: Longman Cheshire.

Goddard, V. and White, B. (1982) 'Child workers and capitalist development', *Development and Change* 13 (4): 465–77.

Goldstein, M.C. and Beall, C.M. (1994) *Odyssey: Mongolian Nomads in the Gobi*, London: Hodder and Stoughton.

Goodnow, J. and Collins, A. (1990) *Development According to Parents: The Nature, Sources and Consequences of Parent's Ideas*, London: Lawrence Erlbaum.

Gordon, L. (1989) *Heroes of Their Own Lives: The Politics and History of Family Violence*, London: Virago Press.

Gough, D. (1996) 'Defining the problem', *Child Abuse and Neglect*, 20, 11: 993–1002.

Government of Mongolia, (with the help of UNICEF) (1993) *Mongolia's National Programme of Action for the Development of Children in the 1990s*, Mongolia: Government of Mongolia.

Grimshaw, J. (1986) *Feminist Philosophers*, Brighton: Harvester Press.

Harden, J. and Scott, S. (1998) *Risk Anxiety and the Social Construction of Childhood*, paper presented at the International Sociological Association World Congress, Montreal, July 1998.

Harkness, S. and Super, C. (1996) *Parents' Cultural Belief Systems: Their Origin, Expressions and Consequences*, London and New York: The Guildford Press.

Hart, R. (1997) *Children's Participation*, London: UNICEF and Earthscan.

Henwood, K., Griffin, C. and Phoenix, A. (eds) (1998) *Standpoints and Differences: Essays in the Practice of Feminist Psychology*, London: Sage.

Hillman, M., Adams, J. and Whitelegg, J. (1990) *One False Move: A Study of Children's Independent Mobility*, London: Policy Studies Institute.

Hockey, J. and James, A. (1993) *Growing Up and Growing Old: Aging and Dependency in the Life Course*, London: Sage.

Holst, J., Kruchov, N., Madsen, U. and Norgaard, E. (1996) *School Development in Mongolia 1992–4*, Copenhagen: Royal Danish School of Educational Studies.

Honig, M.-S. (1996) 'Normative Implikationen der Kindheitsforschung', *Zeitschrift für Sozialisationsforschung und Erziehungssoziologie* 16: 9–25.

Honig, M.-S. (1999) *Entwurf einer Theorie der Kindheit*, Frankfurt am Main: Suhrkamp.

Hood, S., Kelley, P. and Mayall, B. (1996) 'Children as research subjects: A risky enterprise', *Children and Society*, 10: 117–28.

Humphrey, C., with Onon, U. (1996) *Shamans and Elders: Experience, Knowledge and Power among the Deau Mongols*, Oxford: Clarendon.

Hutchby, I. and Moran-Ellis, J. (1998a) 'Situating children's social competence', in I. Hutchby and J. Moran-Ellis (eds) *Children and Social Competence*, London: Falmer.

Hutchby, I. and Moran-Ellis, J. (eds) (1998b) *Children and Social Competence*, London: Falmer.

Jaeger, H. (1977) 'Generationen in der Geschichte: Überlegungen zu einer umstrittenen Konzeption', *Geschichte und Gesellschaft*, 4: 429–52.

James, A. and Prout, A. (1995) 'Hierarchy, boundary and agency: Toward a theoretical perspective on childhood', *Sociological Studies of Children*, 7: 77–99.

James, A. and Prout, A. (1997) 'Re-presenting childhood: Time and transition in the study of childhood', in A. James and A. Prout (eds) *Constructing and Reconstructing Childhood: Contemporary Issues in the Sociological Study of Childhood*, Second Edition, London: Falmer.

James, A. and Prout, A. (eds) (1990) *Constructing and Reconstructing Childhood: Contemporary Issues in the Sociological Study of Childhood*, London: Falmer Press.

James, A., Jenks, C. and Prout, A. (1998) *Theorizing Childhood*, Cambridge: Polity Press.

John, M. (ed.) (1996) *Children in Charge: The Child's Right to a Fair Hearing*, London: Jessica Kingsley.

Jurczyk, K. and Rerrich, M.S. (1993) (eds) *Die Arbeit des Alltags: Beiträge zu einer Soziologie der alltäglichen Lebensführung*, Freiburg: Lambertus.

Kagitcibasi, C. (1996) *Family and Human Development: A View from the Other Side*, New Jersey: Lawrence Erlbaum.

Katz, E. (1991) 'Breaking the myth of harmony: Theoretical and methodological guidelines to the study of rural third world households', *Review of Radical Political Economies* 23 (3 & 4): 37–56.

Katz, I. (1995) 'Approaches to empowerment and participation in child protection', in C. Cloke and M. Davies (eds), *Participation and Empowerment in Child Protection*, Chichester: John Wiley and Sons.

Kellerhals, J. and Montandon, C. (1991) *Les Stratégies Éducatives des Familles*, Paris: Delachaux and Niestlé.

Kelley, P., Mayall, B. and Hood, S. (1997) 'Children's accounts of risk', *Childhood*, 4, 3: 305–24.

Kempe, R. and Kempe, C. (1978) *Child Abuse*, London: Fontana/Open Books.

Kertzer, D. I. (1983) 'Generation as a sociological problem', *Annual Review of Sociology*, 9: 125–49.

Kirchhöfer, D. (1998) *Aufwachsen in Ostdeutschland*, Weinheim and München: Juventa.

Koppetsch, C. and Burkhart, G. (1999) *Die Illusion der Emanzipation. Zur Wirksamkeit latenter Geschlechtsnormen im Milieuvergleich*, Konstanz: Universitätsverlag Konstanz.

Lattimore, O. (1941) *Mongol Journeys*, London: Jonathan Cape.

Layder, D. (1997) *Modern Social Theory: Key Debates and New Directions*, London: University College London Press.

Leach, P. (1994) *Children First*, London: Penguin.

Liebau, E. and Wulf, C. (1996) 'Einleitung', in E. Liebau and C. Wulf (eds) *Generation*, Weinheim: Deutscher Studienverlag.

Lincoln, Y. (1993) 'I and thou: Method, voice and roles in research with the silenced', in D. McLaughlin and W. Tierney (eds) *Naming Silenced Lives: Personal Narratives and the Process of Educational Change*, London: Routledge.

Lukes, S. (1974) *Power, A Radical View*, London: Macmillan.

Lukes, S. (1986) *Power*, Oxford: Blackwell.

MacKinnon, L. (1998) *Trust and Betrayal in the Treatment of Child Abuse*, New York: Guildford Press.

Makrinotti, D. (1994) 'Conceptualisation of childhood in a welfare state: A critical reappraisal', in J. Qvortrup, M. Bardy, G. Sgritta and H. Wintersberger (eds) *Childhood Matters: Social Theory, Practice and Politics*, Aldershot: Avebury.

Manicas, P. (1998) 'A realist social science', in M. Archer, R. Bhaskar, A. Collier, T. Lawson and A. Norrie (eds) *Critical Realism: Essential Readings*, London: Routledge.

Mannheim, K. (1952 [1928]) 'The problem of generations', *Essays in the Sociology of Knowledge*, London: Routledge and Kegan Paul.

Mason, J. and Noble-Spruell, C. (1993) 'Child protection policy in New South Wales: A critical analysis', in J. Mason (ed.) *Child Welfare Policy: Critical Australian Perspectives*, Sydney: Hale & Iremonger.

Mason, J. and Steadman, B. (1997) 'The significance of the conceptualisation of childhood for protection policy', *Family Matters*, 46: 31–6.

Matthes, J. (1985) 'Karl Mannheims "Das Problem der Generationen", neu gelesen: Generationen-"Gruppen" oder "gesellschaftliche Regelung von Zeitlichkeit"?', *Zeitschrift für Soziologie*, 14, 5: 363–72.

Matthews, G.B. (1994) *The Philosophy of Childhood*, Cambridge, Mass.: Harvard University Press.

Mayall, B. (1994a) *Negotiating Health: Children at Home and Primary School*, London: Cassell.

Mayall, B. (ed.) (1994b) *Children's Childhoods: Observed and Experienced*, London: Falmer Press.

Mayall, B. (1996) *Children, Health and the Social Order*, Buckingham: Open University Press.

Mayall, B. (1998) 'Children, emotions and daily life at home and school', in G. Bendelow and S. Williams (eds) *Emotions in Social Life*, London: Routledge.

McLelland, R. (1998) 'Summary of submission received by the Joint Standing Committee on Treaties, Inquiry into the status of the United Nations Convention on the Rights of the Child in Australia', Sydney: Paper Presented to National Children's Summit 'Frameworks for the Future'. Policy Pre-Summit Forum.

Meyer, S. and Schulze, E. (1994) *Alles automatisch – Technikfolgen für Familien. Längsschnittanalysen und zukünftige Entwicklung*, Berlin: edition sigma.

Mies, M. (1991) 'Women's research or feminist research?', in M. Fonow and J. Cook (eds) *Beyond Methodology, Feminist Scholarship as Lived Research*, Bloomington: Indiana University Press.

Milkie, M.A., Simon, R.W. and Powell, B. (1997) 'Through the eyes of children: youths' perceptions and evaluations of maternal and paternal roles', *Social Psychological Quarterly*, 60, 3: 218–37.

Ministry of Enlightenment, Mongolia (1996) *Mongolia Education Statistics 1995–6*, Mongolia: Ministry of Enlightenment.

Mischau, A., Blättel-Mink, B. and Kramer, C. (1998) 'Innerfamiliale Arbeiteilung – Frauen zwischen Wunsch und Wirklichkeit', *Soziale Welt* 49: 333–54.

Monbiot, G. (1994) *No Man's Land*, London: Macmillan.

Mongolian National University (1994) *Mongolia Demographic Survey: Main Report*, Mongolian National University: Population and Teaching Research Centre.

Montandon, C. (1996) 'Processus de Socialisation et Vécu Émotionnel des Enfants', *Revue Française de Sociologie*, XXXVII: 263–85.

Montandon, C. (1997) *L'Éducation du Point de Vue des Enfants*, Paris: L'Harmattan.

Montandon, C. (1998) 'La Sociologie de l'Enfance: L'essor des travaux en langue anglaise', *Éducation et Sociétés*, 2: 91–118.

Morgan, D.H.J. (1999) *Family Connections*, Cambridge: Polity Press.

Morrow, V. (1994) 'Responsible children? Aspects of children's work and employment outside school in contemporary UK', in B. Mayall (ed.) *Children's Childhoods: Observed and Experienced*, London: Falmer Press.

Morrow, V. (1996) 'Rethinking childhood dependency: Children's contributions to the domestic economy', *The Sociological Review*, 44: 58–77.

National Statistical Board, Mongolia (1996) *Mongolia Household Income and Expenditure Statistics 1995–6 (sample data only)*, Mongolia: National Statistical Board.

National Stepfamily Association (1998) *Facts and Figures*, London: National Stepfamily Association.

New South Wales Child Protection Council (1998) *Having a Say*, Sydney: New South Wales Child Protection Council.

Oakley, A. (1974) *The Sociology of Housework*, London: Robertson.

Onon, U. (1972) *My Childhood in Mongolia*, Oxford: Oxford University Press.

Orellana, M. and Thorne, B. (1998) 'Year-round schools and the politics of time', *Anthropology and Education Quarterly*, 29: 446–72.

Ostner, I. (1978) *Beruf und Hausarbeit. Die Arbeit der Frau in unserer Gesellschaft*, Frankfurt am Main, New York: Campus.

Otter, L. (1986) 'Domestic violence: A feminist perspective: implications for practice', in H. Marchant and B. Wearing (eds) *Gender Reclaimed. Women in Social Work*, Sydney: Hale and Iremonger.

Owen, J. (1996) *Every Childhood Lasts a Lifetime*, Australia: Australian Association of Young People in Care.

Pasquale, J. (1998) *Die Arbeit der Mütter. Verberuflichung und Professionalisierung moderner Mutterabeit*, München: Juventa, Weinheim.

Peterson, G.W. and Rollins, B.C. (1987) 'Parent-child socialization', in M.B. Sussmann and J.K. Steimetz (eds) *Handbook of Marriage and the Family*, New York: Plenum Press.

Pfau-Effinger, B. (1993) 'Modernisation, culture and part-time work', in *Work, Employment and Society*, 7: 383–410.

Pfau-Effinger, B. (1996) 'Analyse internationaler Differenzen in der Erwerbsbeteilgung von Frauen', *Kölner Zeitschrift für Soziologie und Sozialpsychologie,* 48: 462–92.

Pilcher, J. (1994) 'Mannheim's sociology of generations: An undervalued legacy', *British Journal of Sociology*, 45, 3: 481–95.

Pilcher, J. (1995) *Age and Generation in Modern Britain*, Oxford: Oxford University Press.

Pilcher J. and Wagg S. (eds) (1996) *Thatcher's Children: Politics, Childhood and Society in the 1980s and 1990s*, London: Falmer.

Pollard, A. (1985) *The Social World of the Primary School*, London: Holt, Rinehart and Wilson.

Pollard, A. (1996) *The Social World of Children's Learning*, London: Cassell.

Pollard, A., Broadfoot, P., Croll, P., Osborn, M. and Abbot, D. (1994) *Changing English Primary Schools,* London: Cassell.

Porpora, D.V. (1998) 'Four concepts of social structure', in M. Archer, R. Bhaskar, A. Collier, T. Lawson and A. Norrie (eds) *Critical Realism: Essential Readings*, London: Routledge.

Pourtois, J.P. and Desmet, H. (1989) 'L'Éducation familiale', *Revue Française de Pédagogie*, 86: 69–101.

Preuss-Lausitz, U., Büchner, P., Fischer-Kowalski, M., Geulen, D., Karsten, M.E., Kulke, C., Rabe-Kleberg, U., Thunemeyer, B., Schütze, Y., Seidl, P., Zeiher, H. and

Zimmermann, P. (1983) *Kriegskinder, Konsumkinder, Krisenkinder: Zur Sozialisations-geschichte seit dem Zweiten Weltkrieg,* Weinheim and Basel: Beltz.

Pross, H. (1975) *Die Wirklichkeit der Hausfrau,* Reinbeck: Rowohlt.

Punch, S. (1998) 'Negotiating independence: Children and young people growing up in rural Bolivia', Unpublished PhD thesis, University of Leeds.

Punch, S. (1999) 'Pig watching and potato peeling: Hierarchies of work for children in rural Bolivia', Paper presented at the Conference for European Sociological Association, Amsterdam, August 1999.

Punch, S. (2000) 'Children's strategies for creating playspaces: Negotiating independence in rural Bolivia', in S. Holloway and G. Valentine (eds) *Children's Geographies: Living, Playing, Learning and Transforming Everyday Worlds,* London: Routledge.

Punch, S. (forthcoming 2001) 'Multiple methods and research relations with children in rural Bolivia', in C. Dwyer and M. Limb (eds) *Qualitative Methodologies for Geographers,* London: Arnold.

Qvortrup, J. (1994) 'Introduction', in J. Qvortrup, M. Bardy, G. Sgritta and H. Wintersberger (eds) *Childhood Matters: Social Theory, Practice and Politics,* Aldershot: Avebury.

Qvortrup, J. (2000) 'Macro-analysis of childhood', in P. Christensen and A. James (eds) *Research with Children: Perspectives and Practices,* London and New York: Falmer Press.

Rayner, M. (1995) 'Children's rights in Australia', in B. Franklin (ed.) *The Handbook of Children's Rights,* London: Routledge.

Rayner, M. (1996) 'Self, self-esteem and sense of place: an Australian framework for children's rights claims in the 1990s', in K. Funder (ed.) *Citizen Child: Australian Law and Children's Rights,* Melbourne: Australian Institute of Family Studies.

Rerrich, M.S. (1983) 'Veränderte Elternschaft. Entwicklungen in der familialen Arbeit mit Kindern seit 1950', *Soziale Welt,* 34: 420–49.

Reynolds, P. (1991) *Dance Civet Cat: Child Labour in the Zambezi Valley,* Athens, Ohio: Ohio University Press.

Ribbens, J. (1994) *Mothers and their Children: A Feminist Sociology of Child Rearing,* London: Sage.

Ribbens, J., Edwards, R. and Gillies, V. (1999) *Parenting and Step-parenting: Contemporary Moral Tales,* Occasional Paper 4, Centre for Family and Household Research, Oxford: Oxford Brookes University.

Rosaldo, R. (1993) *Culture and Truth: The Remaking of Social Analysis,* London: Routledge.

Rosenbaum, H. (1982) *Soziologie der Familie,* Frankfurt am Main: Surhkamp.

Ryder, N. B. (1965) 'The cohort as a concept in the study of social change', *American Sociological Review,* 30: 843–61.

Sachs, W. (1992) *The Development Dictionary,* London: Zed Books.

Saporiti, A. (1994) 'A methodology to make children count', in J. Qvortrup, M. Bardy, G. Sgritta and H. Wintersberger (eds) *Childhood Matters: Social Theory, Practice and Politics,* Aldershot: Avebury.

Sayer, A. (1992) *Method in Social Science,* London: Routledge.

Schildkrout, E. (1981) 'The employment of children in Kano (Nigeria)', in G. Rodgers and G. Standing (eds) *Child Work, Poverty and Underdevelopment,* Geneva: International Labour Organisation.

Scott, J. (1998) 'Relationism, cubism and reality: beyond relativism', in T. May and M. Williams (eds) *Knowing the Social Worlds,* Buckingham: Open University Press.

Sgritta, G. (1994) 'The generational division of welfare: Equity and conflict', in J. Qvortrup, M. Bardy, G. Sgritta and H. Wintersberger (eds) *Childhood Matters: Social Theory, Practice and Politics,* Aldershot: Avebury.

Shamgar-Handelman, L. (1994) 'To who does childhood belong?', in J. Qvortrup, M. Bardy, G. Sgritta and H Wintersberger (eds) *Childhood Matters: Social Theory, Practice and Politics*, Aldershot: Avebury.

Sherman, A. (1996) *Rules, Routines and Regimentation*, Nottingham: Educational Heretics Press.

Shilling, C. (1992) 'Reconceptualising structure and agency in the sociology of education: structuration, theory and schooling', *British Journal of Sociology of Education*, 13, 1: 69–87.

Sinclair, R. (ed.) (1996) *Children and Society*, Special edition on research with children, 10, 2.

Sluckin, A. (1981) *Growing Up in the Playground*, London: Routledge and Kegan Paul.

Smith, D.E. (1988) *The Everyday World as Problematic: A Feminist Sociology*, Milton Keynes: Open University Press.

Smith, D.E. (1999) *Writing the Social: Critique, Theory and Investigations*, Toronto: University of Toronto Press.

Solberg, A. (1990) 'Negotiating childhood: Changing constructions of age for Norwegian children', in A. James and A. Prout (eds) *Constructing and Reconstructing Childhood. Contemporary Issues in the Sociological Study of Childhood*, London: Falmer Press.

Stainton-Rogers, R. and Stainton-Rogers, W. (1992) *Stories of Childhood: Shifting Agendas of Child Concern*, London and New York: Harvester Wheatsheaf.

Swartz, D. (1997) *Culture and Power: The Sociology of Pierre Bourdieu*, Chicago: University of Chicago Press.

Therborn, G. (1995) *European Modernity and Beyond: The Trajectory of European Societies 1945–2000*, London: Sage.

Thomas, N. and O'Kane, C. (1999) 'Experiences of decision-making in middle childhood: The example of children "looked after" by local authorities', *Childhood*, 6, 3: 369–88

Thorpe, D. (1994) *Evaluating Child Protection*, Buckingham: Open University Press.

Triggs, P. and Pollard, A. (1998) 'Pupil experience and a curriculum for life-long learning', in C. Richards and P. H. Taylor (eds) *How Shall we School Our Children? Primary Education and its Future*, London: Falmer.

Turner, B.S. (1999) *Classical Sociology*, London: Sage.

Wa Thiongi'o, N. (1993) *Moving the Centre: The Struggle for Cultural Freedoms*, London: Heinemann.

Waksler, F.C. (1991a) 'The hard times of childhood and children's strategies for dealing with them', in F.C. Waksler (ed.) *Studying the Social Worlds of Children: Sociological Readings*, London: Falmer Press.

Waksler, F.C. (1991b) *Studying the Social Worlds of Children: Sociological Readings*, London: Falmer Press.

Waksler, F.C. (1991c) 'Studying children: Phenomenological insights', in F.C. Waksler (ed.) *Studying the Social Worlds of Children: Sociological Readings*, London: Falmer Press.

Waksler, F.C. (1996) *The Little Trials of Childhood and Children's Strategies for Dealing with Them*, London: Falmer Press.

Walkerdine, V. and Lucey, H. (1989) *Democracy in the Kitchen: Regulating Mothers and Socialising Daughters,* London: Virago.

Wartofsky, M. (1983) 'The child's construction of the world and the world's construction of the child: from historical epistemology to historical psychology', in F.S. Kessel and A.W. Siegel (eds) *The Child and Other Cultural Inventions*, New York: Praeger.

Weber, M. (1956) *Wirtschaft und Gesellschaft. Grundriß der verstehenden Soziologie,* Köln und Berlin: Kiepenheuer und Witsch.

Weber, M. (1968 [1922]) *Economy and Society,* Berkeley, Calif.: University of California Press.

Wilkinson, R. (1994) *Unfair Shares: The Effects of Widening Income Difference on the Welfare of the Young,* London: Barnardos.

Willis, P. (1977) *Learning to Labour,* Farnborough: Saxon.

Wintersberger, H. (1996) 'The ambivalence of modern childhood: A plea for a European strategy for children', in W. Wintersberger (ed.) *Children on the Way from Marginality to Citizenship: Childhood Policies: Conceptual and Practical Issues,* Eurosocial Report 61, Vienna: European Centre.

Woods, P. (1979) *The Divided School,* London: Routledge and Kegan Paul.

World Bank (1996) *Mongolia: Poverty in a Transition Economy, Draft Report,* Rural and Social Development Operations Division, Chinese and Mongolia Department, East Asia and Pacific Regional Office.

Wright, E.O. (1985) *Classes,* London: Verso.

Wright, E.O. (1989) 'Rethinking once again, the concept of class structure', in E.O. Wright (ed.) *The Debate on Classes,* London: Verso.

Wright, E.O. (1996) 'Marxism after Communism', in S.T. Turner (ed.) *Social Theory and Sociology: The Classics and Beyond,* Cambridge/Oxford: Blackwell.

Wright, E.O. (1997) *Class Counts,* Cambridge: Cambridge University Press.

Youniss, J. (1980) *Parents and Peers in Social Development,* Chicago: University of Chicago Press.

Zeiher, H. (2000) 'Hausarbeit: Zur Integration der Kinder in die häusliche Arbeitsteilung', in H. Hengst and H. Zeiher (eds) *Die Arbeit der Kinder: Kindheitskonzept und Arbeitsteilung zwischen den Generationen,* Weinheim und München: Juventa.

Zeiher, H.J. and Zeiher, H. (1994) *Orte und Zeiten der Kinder. Soziales Leben im Alltag von Großstadtkindern,* Weinheim und München: Juventa.

Zelizer, V. (1985) *Pricing the Priceless Child,* New York: Basic Books.

Index

An environmentally friendly book printed and bound in England by www.printondemand-worldwide.com

PEFC Certified

This product is
from sustainably
managed forests
and controlled
sources

www.pefc.org

PEFC/16-33-415

FSC
www.fsc.org

MIX
Paper from
responsible sources
FSC® C004959

This book is made entirely of sustainable materials; FSC paper for the cover and PEFC paper for the text pages.

#0318 - 031214 - C0 - 234/156/11 - PB